the complete BANNER handbook

A creative guide for banner design & construction

By
Janet Litherland

Meriwether Publishing Ltd., Publisher
P.O. Box 7710
Colorado Springs, CO 80933

Editors: Michelle Gallardo, Arthur L. Zapel
Typesetting: Sharon Garlock
Cover design and illustrations: Michelle Gallardo

Printed in the United States of America
First Edition

Library of Congress Cataloging-in-Publication Data

Litherland, Janet.
The complete banner handbook.

1. Flags. 2. Wall hangings. I. Title.
II. Title: Banner handbook.
TT850.2.L57 1987 746.3 87-71778
ISBN 0-916260-48-8

for Wil and Kay,

my "banner parents"

CONTENTS

Chapter 1:
Banners Through the Ages **3**
Flags and Heraldry; Tapestries

Chapter 2:
Banners for Today **7**
Purposes, Uses, Sizes, Shapes

Chapter 3:
Symbols **19**
Biblical Use, Color Symbolism, Universal Symbols, Crosses, Stars, Candles, Trees, Flowers, Branches, Fruit, Living Creatures, Sacred Monograms, Combination Symbols, Shields of the Apostles

Chapter 4:
Designing Banners **41**
Inspiration, Creativity, Lettering, Composition, Color

Chapter 5:
Constructing Banners **53**
Patterns, Materials, Preparation, Assembly, Finishing, Hanging, Mounting, Displaying

Chapter 6:
Special Techniques **67**
Appliqué and Embroidery, Stuffing, Batik, Tie-Dyeing

Chapter 7:
Computer Banners **75**
Trends, Techniques

Chapter 8:
Ideas Plus **85**
ABC Christmas Banners, Scripture Banners, Music Banners, Choral Reading Banners, Family Banners, Group Banners, Special-use Banners, Odds 'n Ends Banners, "Think on These Things"

Other books and reference guides by Janet Litherland:

The Clown Ministry Handbook
Let's Move
Let's Move Again!
The Wonderful Art of Storytelling
Youth Ministry From Start To Finish

INTRODUCTION

It has been our pleasure over the past decade to work with art designers, writers and educators to develop a continuing line of unique banner kits for liturgical programs, church and school decoration and similar art-related activities. Letters and photos have reached our office from just about every state in the union and several foreign countries. Through them we discovered that banners speak a universal language. Banners permit us to beautifully celebrate an idea or thought important to us.

With this discovery came the realization that we could never design and publish enough banner kits to express the inspired statements of everyone and that a practical, instructional book was needed for those who wanted to create their own banners. We then immediately commissioned Janet Litherland to research, organize and write what we believe is the first and only comprehensive book on banner making. Her wide-ranging credits as a specialist writer on many subjects assured us that this reference edition would be the very best current work on the subject. We believe that the extensive research represented by these pages will convince you that our mission has been a success.

The Publisher

Chapter 1

Banners Through the Ages

Picture a sunset . . . a sunrise . . . a swirl of fluffy white clouds . . . a starlit sky . . . a rainbow. These are God's banners. They signify his wonder, majesty, and mystery. They are banners of inspiration, which he changes continually, offering each person in the world a picture of hope, a new beginning. All one has to do is look at them!

Wouldn't it be wonderful to be able to create such banners of blessing, banners that could warm cold hearts, heal broken ones, and stimulate those that barely beat? The visual impact! On a small but human scale we can achieve it. At least we can try, as humankind has tried from the very beginning.

Banners are rooted in symbols, and because of this our earthly banners can be traced to earliest times, to the drawings etched into cave walls for future generations to see and understand. Banners are more than decorations. They *signify* something. They communicate.

The first banners resembling those we use today were carried by the Egyptians in 5,000 B.C. Yes, that long ago! The men attached long streamers to poles and carried them into battle as a plea to their gods for assistance. Romans attached their banners to spears. This streamer type of banner was also flown from ships and later placed on the embattlements of forts to demonstrate possession. To lose a banner was considered a great disgrace.

The words "banner" and "standard" in the Old Testament refer to "flags" as we know them today. These began as pieces of carved wood, leather, or metal, which were placed on top of staves and used as a means of identification, either of a person, a family, or a group of people (similar to the totems of North American Indians). Animals were favorite symbols — the Assyrians used the image of a running bull; Persians chose the eagle. These early images were the forerunners of personal heraldry, popular with the knights of the Middle Ages. The first use of personal heraldry is thought to be the Black Lion of Flanders, which was used on the seal of a Count of Flanders in 1164, though there is evidence of the use of such symbols in Numbers 2:2 — "Every man of the children of Israel shall pitch by his own standard, with the ensign of their father's house." Within families, heraldic symbols are passed from generation to generation. Today, unfortunately, they have become symbols of social status.

Tapestries woven of wool, linen, and silk, and often embellished with gold threads, were important to churchfolk of the Middle Ages. The weaving technique was simple and was most often done by monks on primitive looms. Not only were the tapestries lovely to look at, hanging on church walls, they also helped keep out the cold air! In addition, they served as teaching tools for the congregations, most of whom could not read or write. These tapestries inspired the beautiful, embroidered and appliqued banners used in church sanctuaries today.

Religious symbols appeared on standards in Mesopotamian culture about 4,000 years ago, but the cross was first carried on Constantine's banner in the 4th Century. As a symbol, the cross was very important to early Christians, who were persecuted during the Crusades. Their cross-bearing flags served as morale boosters and helped instill strength of spirit within the people.

When Christopher Columbus sailed for America, his personal flag displayed a large cross to represent his mission — the spread of Christianity. Four hundred years later, Charles C. Overton designed the "Christian Flag," still used in churches of all denominations. Of course it contains the red cross, representing the life and death of Jesus and the promise of eternal life. Its blue background represents Jesus' faithfulness, and the large white area symbolizes the purity of Jesus and the joy of mankind.

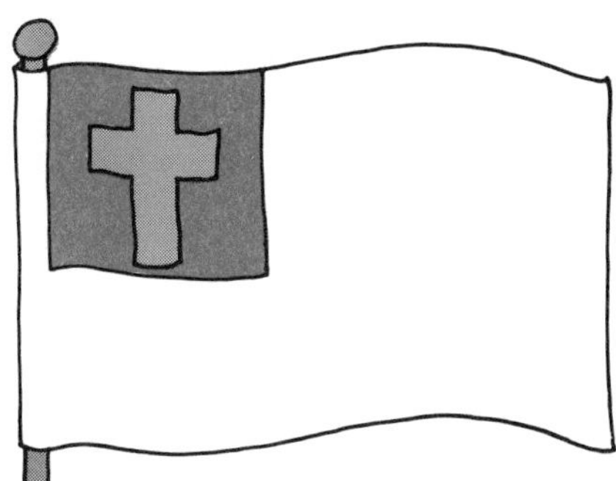

During the French Revolution flags and banners became political symbols, with individuals flying them in support of their country. National flags are strong symbols that evoke strong emotions. Think of the joy and pride we Americans feel at the raising of our own special banner — the "Star-Spangled Banner." George Washington said, "We take the stars from heaven, the red from our mother country, separating it by white stripes, thus showing that we have separated from her, and the white stripes shall go down to posterity representing liberty."

Today, the flags of many countries combine politics and religion with crosses on their national flags: England, Scotland, Ireland, Greece, Switzerland, and others. Israel's flag bears the "Star of David."

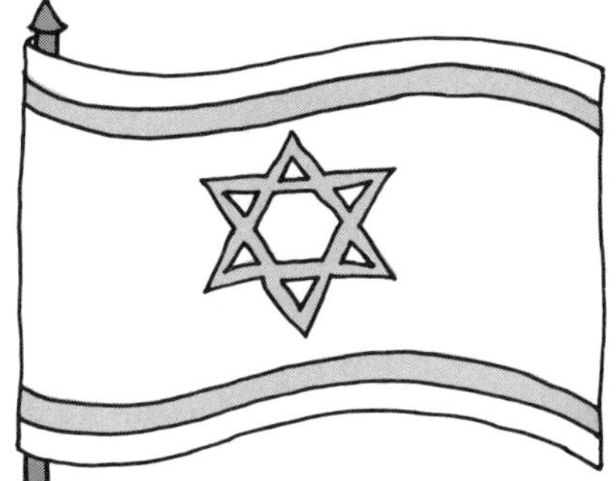

Banners, whether they are called banners, standards, or flags, have always stood for something, have always "packed a punch." From the rainbow that God paints across the sky to the banners of ancient Egyptian soldiers, to the cross-bearing flags of early Christians, to the national symbols waving from tall poles, to the tapestries hanging in church sanctuaries, to the computer banners stretching around a youth fellowship room, banners have been and still are a powerful means of communication. What an opportunity for creation, inspiration and blessing!

> ***"In the name of our God we will set up our banners."*** *(Psalm 20:5)*

Chapter 2

Banners for Today

Technically, a "banner" hangs from a crossbar or is suspended between two poles, though today's banners are often attached to standards or simply pinned to walls.

As in olden times, modern banners must communicate. This is their sole purpose. A single piece of information is presented simply, without clutter, which distinguishes a banner from a poster.

banner

poster

Because banners attract attention, they are particularly useful as advertising or promotion aids.

(Designed by Wil and Kay Comstock, Loudon United Methodist Church, Loudon, Tennessee. Incorporates the United Methodist symbol, the cross and flame. Used for promotion of Methodism.)

Also consider banners as:

- — teaching tools
- — worship aids
- — group identifiers
- — motivators
- — providers of inspiration

As worship aids or teaching tools, banner parts can be prepared in advance and put together during the process of instruction or worship. Parts are later attached permanently, and the banner becomes a wall hanging.

Example:

Many Christian churches observe the four Sundays of Advent by lighting the candles of an Advent Wreath, one each Sunday. Some add a tall white candle to be lit on Christmas Eve or Christmas Day. The circle of greenery symbolizes new life and eternal life; the four lavender candles represent Hope, Peace, Love, and Joy — anticipating the coming of the Messiah; and the tall white candle represents Jesus, the Light of the World. Church families are provided a short litany to read as they light one candle each week. This would be an excellent time for banner ministry, either in place of or in addition to the Advent Wreath. At the close of the season, the church (or Sunday School, or youth group) would then have a permanent Advent Banner for use in future years.

The banner shown on the following page uses purple, the liturgical color of Advent (signifying penitence, preparation, royalty), for the background. The golden sun is a symbol of Jesus' coming: "But unto you that fear my name shall the Sun of righteousness arise with healing in his wings." (Malachi 4:2)

In the center is the purple Tau Cross, also known as the "Prophetic" or "Anticipatory" cross. It is an appropriate symbol for Advent, because it is believed to be the shape of Moses' staff, which he lifted up in the wilderness, and to which Jesus later referred. "And Moses made a serpent of brass, and put it upon a pole, and it came to pass, that if a serpent had bitten any man, when he beheld the serpent of brass, he lived." (Numbers 21:9) "And as Moses lifted up the serpent in the wilderness, even so must the Son of Man be lifted up." (John 3:14)

Instructions:

Prepare the basic banner in advance, eliminating the four rays — Hope, Peace, Love, and Joy. Finish the edges and prepare the top for mounting on a standard. (See Chapter 5 for construction techniques.) Prepare the four rays separately, gluing Velcro to their backs and to the corresponding places on the banner. Use this script during the worship services:

FIRST SUNDAY

Scripture: Isaiah 40:1-5

PARENT:

Today is the first Sunday of Advent. Our banner of royal purple signifies the coming of the Messiah. The sun represents Jesus, the Light of the World, and the Prophetic Cross in the center symbolizes the "lifting up" of Christ that all may have eternal life.

CHILD:

Today we add the ray of Hope to our sun. *(Child attaches symbol.)*

PARENT:

Because the prophets gave us reason to hope, this ray symbolizes the hope of all who wait for the coming of our Lord.

Hymn: "O Come, O Come, Emmanuel"

Another excellent symbolic liturgy banner is "The Epiphany Banner" developed by Arthur L. Zapel, designed by Michelle Gallardo, for use on Epiphany Sunday. The bannerkit includes designs, patterns, and a narrative script for up to 12 laypersons. It is available from Contemporary Drama Service.

HOPE
JOY
HE COMES
PEACE
LOVE

SECOND SUNDAY

Scripture: Isaiah 9:6-7; Luke 2:13-14

PARENT:

Today is the second Sunday of Advent, a day for contemplating the peace of the Promised One. This peace is the peace we feel in our hearts as we live our lives for Jesus. It is the peace made possible the world over, through the coming of the Messiah.

CHILD:

Today we add the ray of Peace to our sun. *(Child attaches symbol.)*

PARENT:

Because the angels promised it, this ray symbolizes peace on earth, the peace available to all who put their trust in the Prince of Peace.

Hymn: "Come, Thou Long Expected Jesus"

THIRD SUNDAY

Scripture: Luke 2:11; John 3:16

PARENT:

Today is the third Sunday of Advent. On this day we recognize the love of God, which came to us in the form of Jesus, his Son. This is truly the Greatest Gift — a baby in a manger at Bethlehem, born to be our Savior.

CHILD:

Today we add the ray of Love to our sun. *(Child attaches symbol.)*

PARENT:

Because God loved the world, he made possible eternal life. It is only fitting that we respond to his love — by loving one another and by loving his Son.

Hymn: "Love Came Down at Christmas"

FOURTH SUNDAY

Scripture: Isaiah 9:2; Luke 2:15-20

PARENT:

Today is the fourth Sunday of Advent. It is time for us to experience, with the shepherds of old, the great joy in receiving the news of the Messiah. The shepherds not only received the news, they believed it!

CHILD:

Today we add the ray of Joy to our sun. *(Child attaches symbol.)*

PARENT:

"Behold, I bring you good tidings of great joy, which shall be to all people. Unto you is born this day in the city of David a Savior, who is Christ the Lord." We have received the news. Will we believe it?
Hymn: "Joy to the World"

The actual *making* of banners also serves a purpose in itself, which is two-fold — fellowship and ministry.

As a group activity, banner-making can't be beat. It provides opportunity for creativity and sharing for all ages. Consider not only youth groups, women's groups, older adult groups, etc., but also the possibility of a mixed-age (intergenerational) group — whoever is interested in making banners. A small group can work on a single banner; a large group, using long tables in a fellowship room, can work on several. As themes and purposes are developed for the banners, work takes on new meaning — group activity becomes group ministry.

Some people prefer to work alone. For them, banner-making is a personal ministry, and this should be encouraged.

With these things in mind, banners are "at home" just about anywhere:

Sunday School, Worship Service, Youth meeting, Wedding, Installation service, Processional, Committee meeting, Banquet/Feast, Concert, Field trip, Confirmation, Women's meeting, Men's meeting, Choir, Funeral, Dedication, Parade, Fellowship supper, Party, Vacation Bible School, Drama ministry, Bar Mitzvah.

Religious seasons and festivals provide plenty of year-round opportunities for banner ministry:

Christian *— Advent, Christmas, Epiphany, Lent, Easter, Ascension, Pentecost.*

Jewish *— Passover (Pesach), Pentecost (Shabuot), New Year's Day (Rosh Hashanah), Day of Atonement (Yom Kippur), Feast of Tabernacles (Sukkot), Purim, Hanukkah, Tisheah B'ab.*

Most churches also celebrate or at least recognize secular holidays, which are excellent times for using banners:

Valentine's Day, Mother's Day, Independence Day, Father's Day, Thanksgiving, Halloween. (Though pagan in origin, Halloween parties, just for fun, are popular with many fellowship groups.)

Inspirational banners are certainly appropriate in the observance of the sacraments:

Protestant *— Baptism, The Lord's Supper.*

Catholic *— Baptism, Confirmation, Eucharist, Penance, Extreme Unction, Marriage, Orders.*

Banners come in many shapes and sizes. They may be small (12" x 18"), medium (24" x 36"), large (6' x 10'), or any size in between. They can also be *very* small (4" x 6") and used as gifts, greetings, tree ornaments, or parts of a mobile.

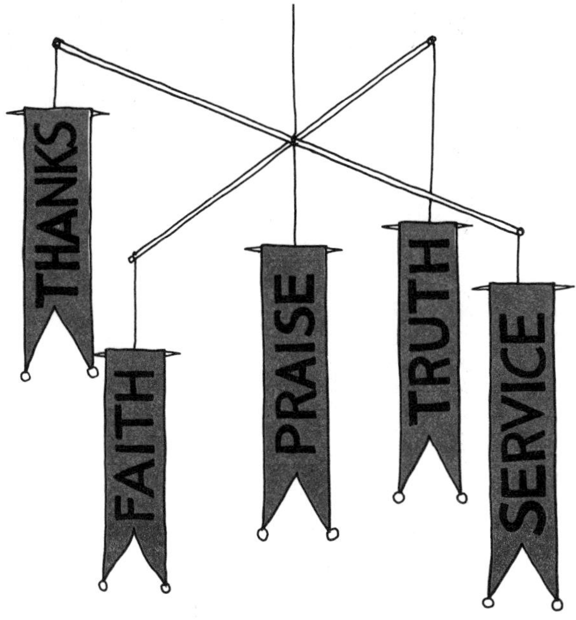

Shapes may be borrowed from the banners of history:

"banderole," a narrow swallowtail

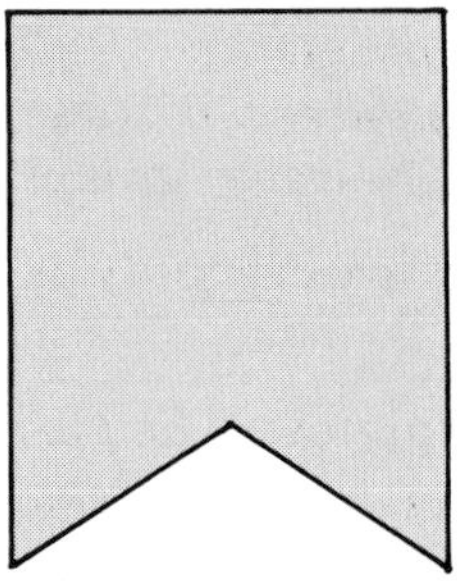

variations of the "gonfalon" from early religious associations of Western Europe

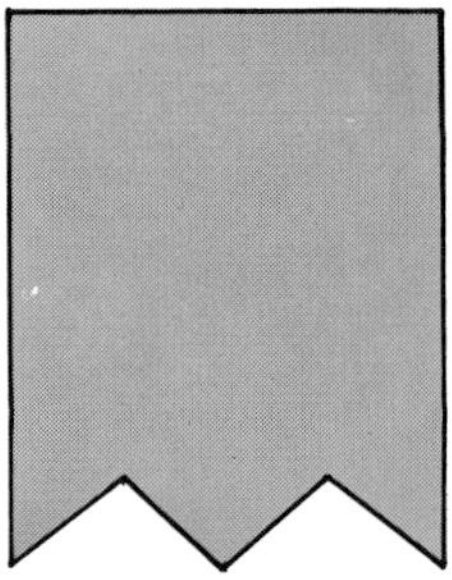

broad swallowtail

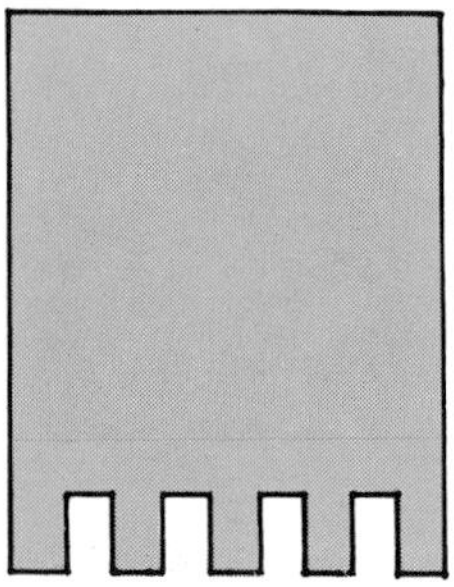

"gonfanon," a war flag of pre-heraldic Western Europe

triple swallowtail

"bannerol," a square

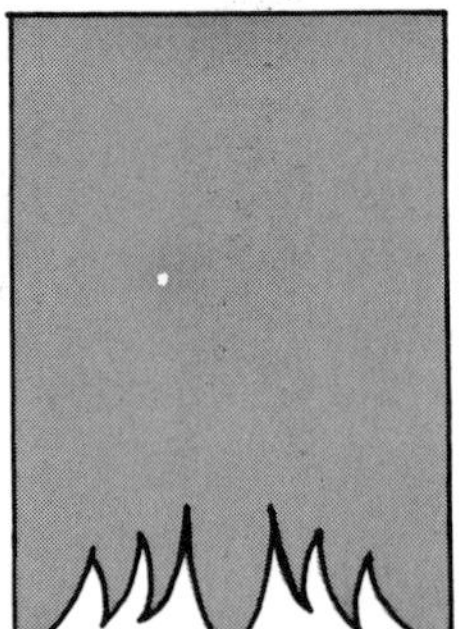

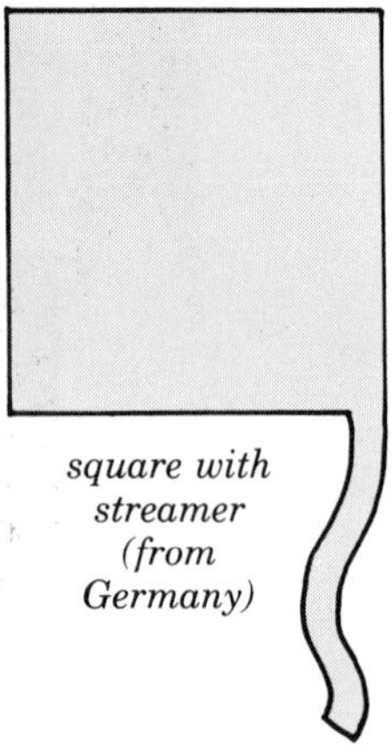

square with streamer (from Germany)

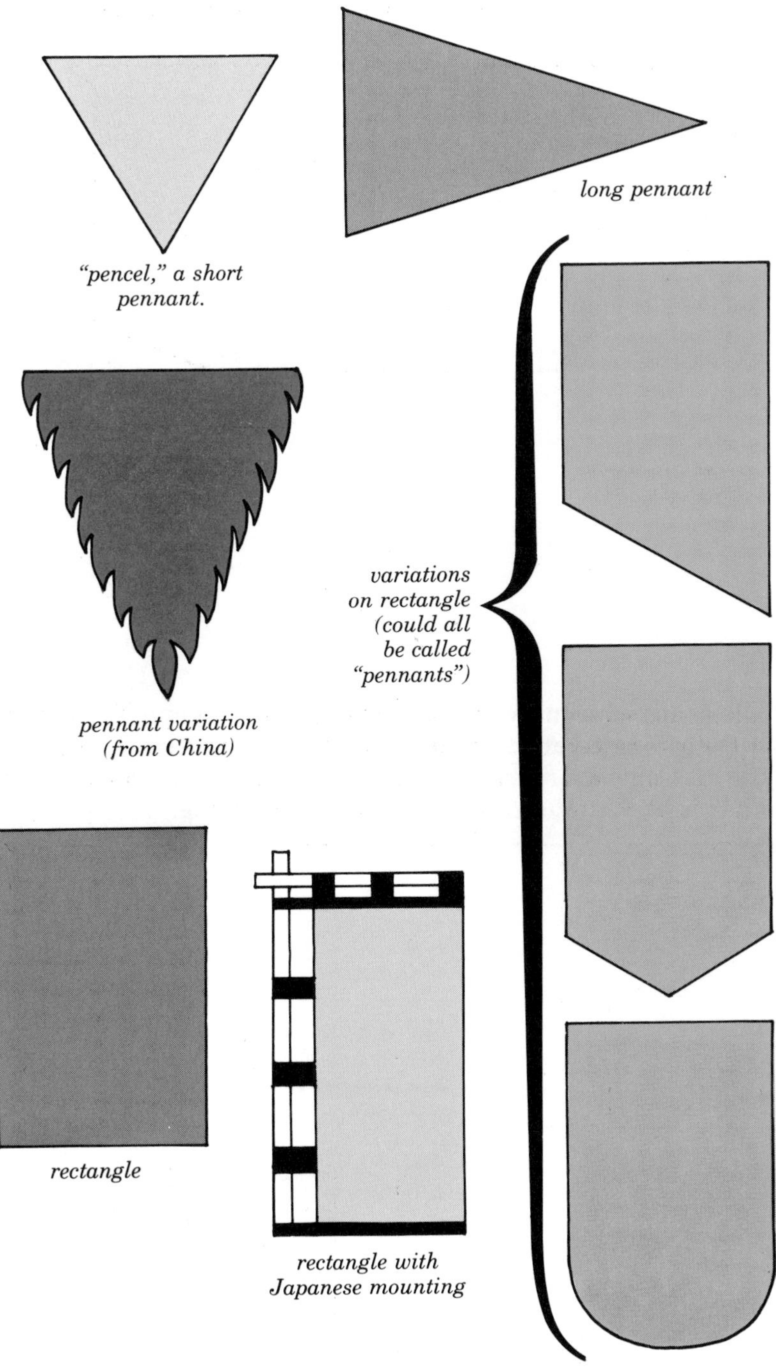

"pencel," a short pennant.
long pennant
pennant variation (from China)
variations on rectangle (could all be called "pennants")
rectangle
rectangle with Japanese mounting

Basic "shield" shapes from heraldry may also be used:

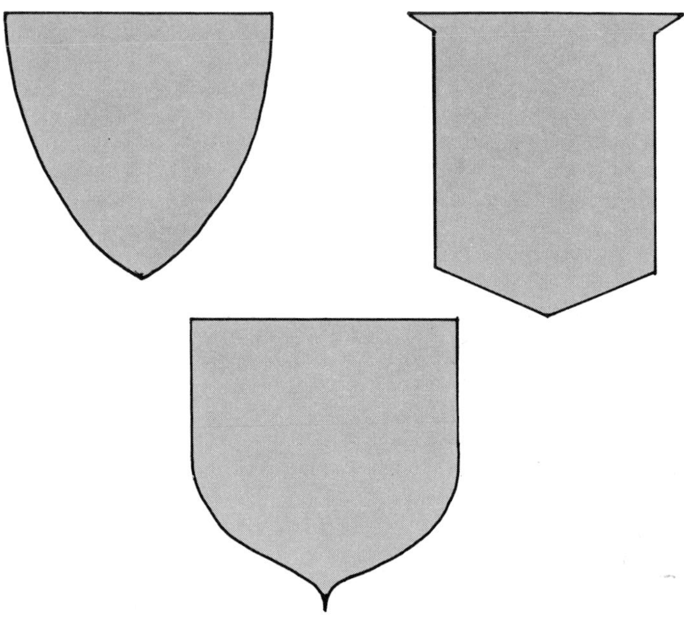

Perhaps someone will want to design a new shape. The important thing to remember is that size and shape must be appropriate to the message and must not detract from it. The purpose of every banner is to communicate one uncluttered theme.

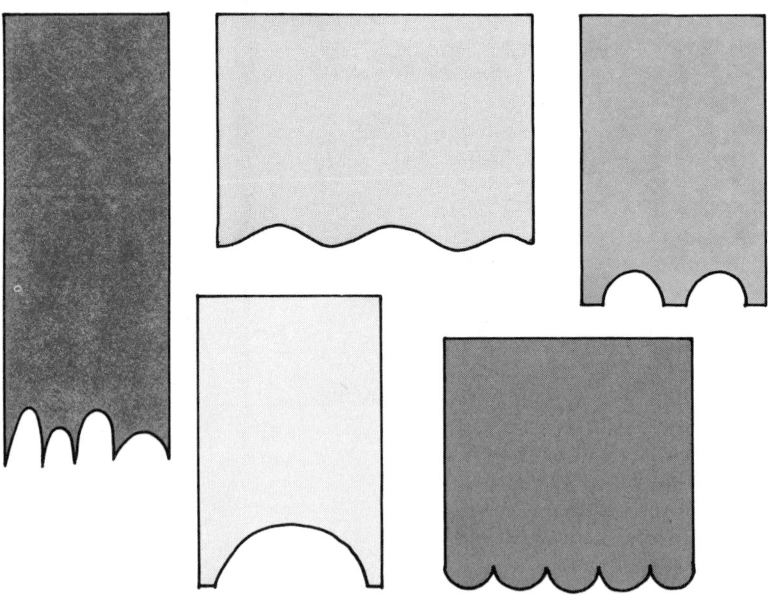

Chapter 3

Symbols

A symbol is something that represents or identifies an abstract idea. It is simple, rather than detailed.

cross = symbol *crucifix = picture*

A wedding ring is a symbol. So is a handshake, a bouquet of flowers, a letter, a word, a number. The skull and crossbones is a symbol, and so is the swastika.

Symbols are everywhere — in doctors' offices, in supermarkets, at golf courses, in parking lots, in school, in elevators. Many tall buildings eliminate a certain symbol, of which the elimination is a symbol in itself — the 13th floor!

The most beautiful symbols, however, are the religious ones.

There are hundreds of them dating back to Old Testament times and earlier. The Bible is rich in symbolism:

The Tree of Life *(Genesis 2:9)*

The Rainbow *(Genesis 9:12-13)*

A Dove *(Genesis 8:11; Matthew 3:16-17)*

The Shepherd *(Psalms 23; John 10:11)*

The Light *(Psalms 27:1; John 8:12; 9:5)*

The Harp and Lyre *(Psalms 33:2-3)*

The Potter's Vessel *(Jeremiah 19)*

The Vine *(Ezekiel 15:2; John 15:5)*

The Salt of the Earth *(Matthew 5:13)*

The Lamb of God *(John 1:29)*

Baptism *(Matthew 3:11)*

The Lord's Supper *(Mark 14:22-25)*

Some people worry about the use of symbols, equating them with the idolatry so abhorred by Old Testament writers.

> ***"Ye shall make you no idols nor graven image, neither rear you up a standing image, neither shall ye set up any image of stone in your land, to bow down unto it: for I am the Lord Your God."*** *(Leviticus 26:1)*

It is true that superstitious use of symbolism led people of the Reformation to the destruction of anything that could be remotely connected to idolatry, including stained glass windows and pipe organs. This was a sorry loss of a great heritage — a severing of belief from which many Protestant groups have never fully recovered. The New Testament affirms what we already know:

> ***"We know that an idol is nothing in the world, and that there is none other God but one."*** *(I Corinthians 8:4)*

It is not the symbol that is important but what it *represents.* We do not worship symbols. They are an aid to worship. In *Our Christian Symbols* Friedrich Rest says, "There is no danger of idolatry when the meaning of a symbol is understood." It is important, therefore, that banners employ symbols that are understood by all who will view them. It may be necessary to educate some congregations in symbolism before symbolic banners are used. *If a banner needs to be explained, it is not a good banner.*

UNIVERSAL SYMBOLS

The Trinity:

three-in-one

circle = eternity

The Father:

the hand of God
(Psalms 139:10)

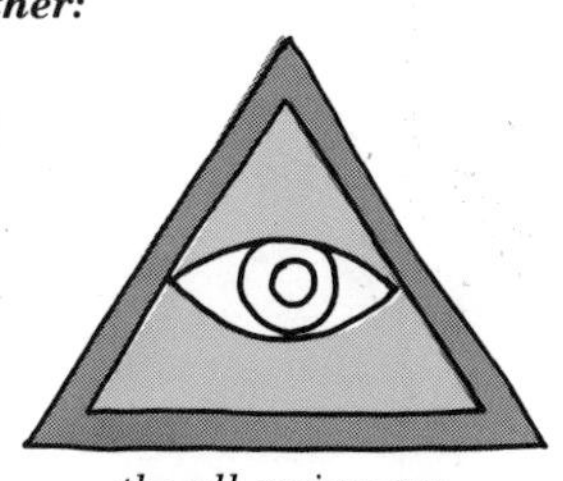

the all-seeing eye
(Psalms 33:18)

The Son:

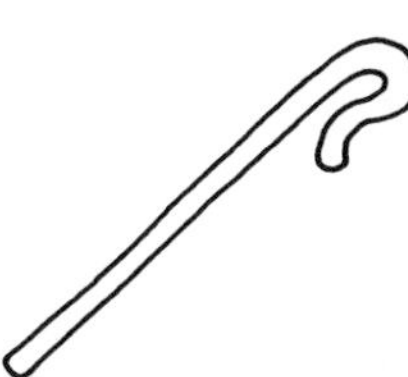

the Good Shepherd
(John 10:11)

the sun of righteousness
(Malachi 4:2)

The Holy Spirit:

descending dove
(Matthew 3:16)

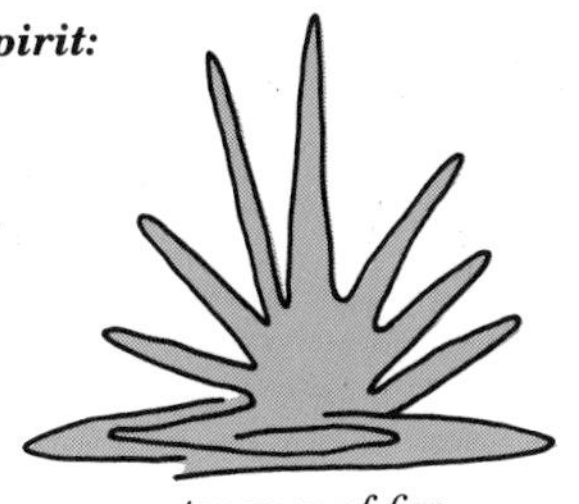

tongues of fire
Pentecost
(Acts 2:3-4)

CROSSES

Tau cross
prophecy cross

Greek cross

Latin cross

Celtic cross
(eternal redemption
through Christ)

Passion cross

St. Andrew's cross

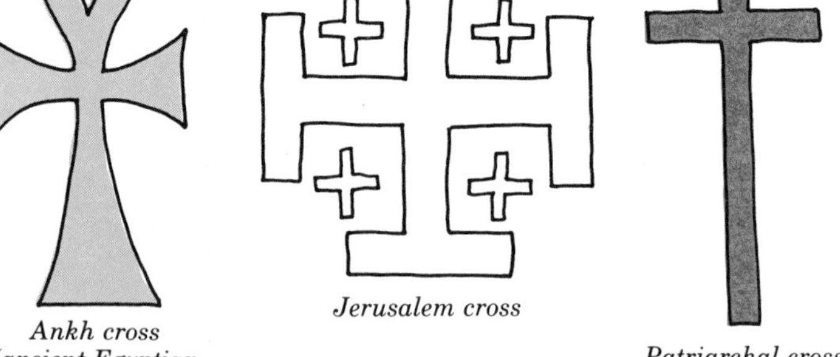

Ankh cross
(ancient Egyptian
symbol of life)

Jerusalem cross

Patriarchal cross

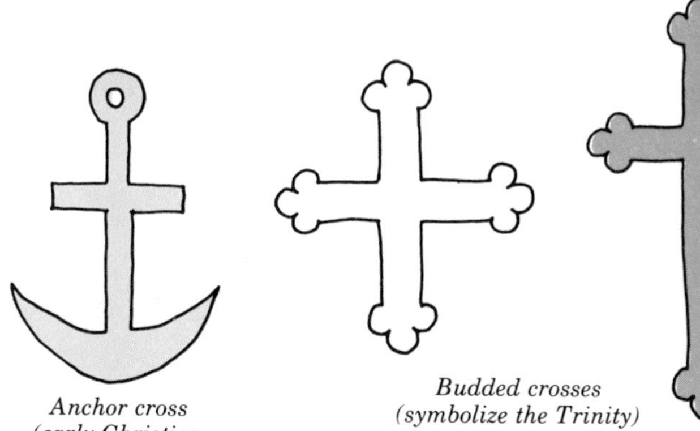

Anchor cross (early Christian symbol of hope)

Budded crosses (symbolize the Trinity)

Calvary cross
Graded cross
(steps = faith, hope, charity)

"The Lenten Cross Banner"
(For a worship celebration. Kit from Contemporary Drama Service contains construction guide and scripts for presentation.)

STARS

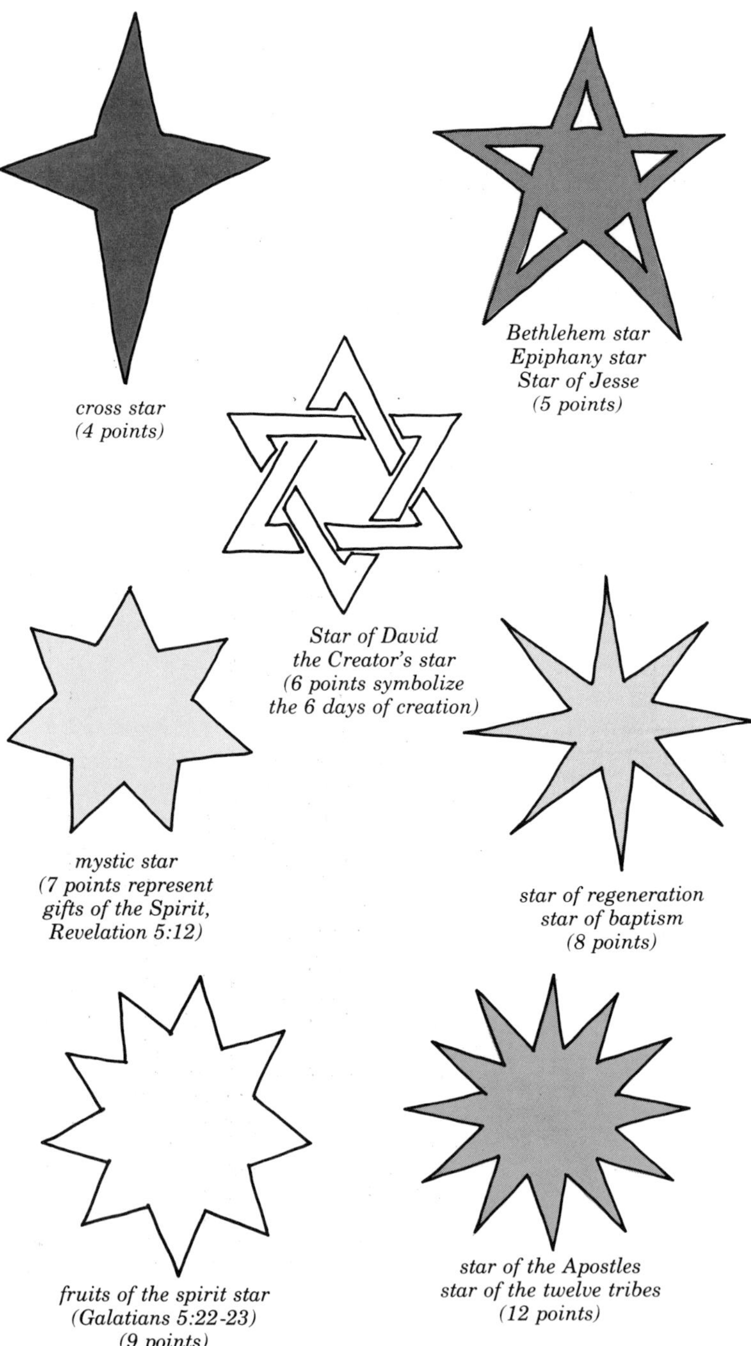
cross star
(4 points)
Bethlehem star
Epiphany star
Star of Jesse
(5 points)
Star of David
the Creator's star
(6 points symbolize
the 6 days of creation)
mystic star
(7 points represent
gifts of the Spirit,
Revelation 5:12)
star of regeneration
star of baptism
(8 points)
fruits of the spirit star
(Galatians 5:22-23)
(9 points)
star of the Apostles
star of the twelve tribes
(12 points)

CANDLES

unity

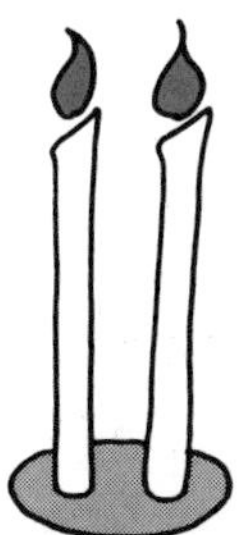
two natures
of Christ
(human-divine)

Trinity

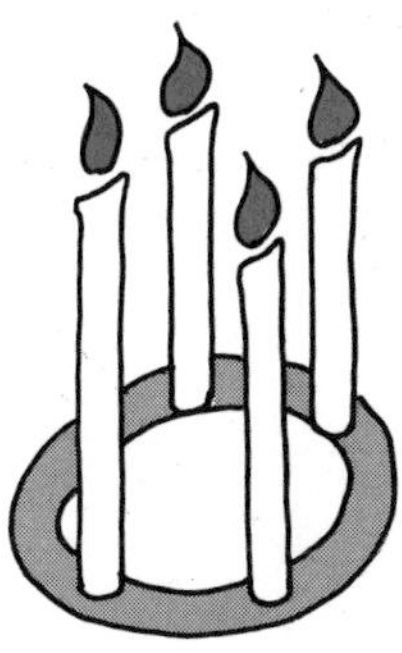
Advent

five wounds
of Christ

seven gifts of the Spirit
the Seven Sacraments

Menorah
Old Testament worship
Jewish symbol of faith

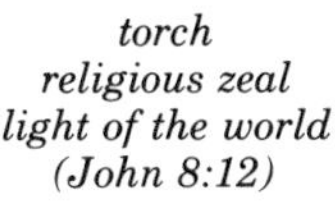
torch
religious zeal
light of the world
(John 8:12)

lamp
"Lamp unto my feet"
(Psalms 119:105)
wisdom, knowledge

TREES, FLOWERS, BRANCHES AND FRUIT

LIVING CREATURES

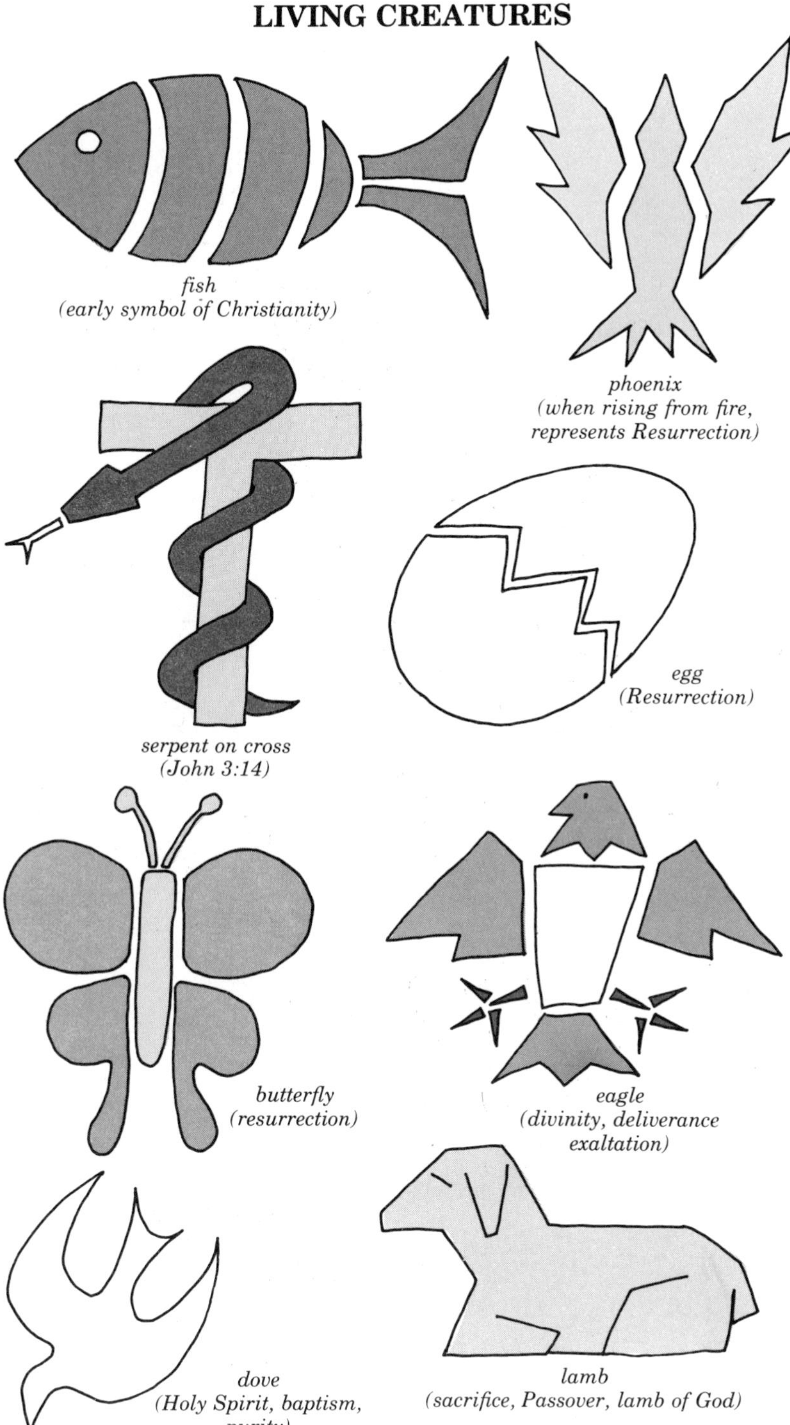

fish
(early symbol of Christianity)

phoenix
(when rising from fire, represents Resurrection)

serpent on cross
(John 3:14)

egg
(Resurrection)

butterfly
(resurrection)

eagle
(divinity, deliverance exaltation)

dove
(Holy Spirit, baptism, purity)

lamb
(sacrifice, Passover, lamb of God)

OTHER SYMBOLS

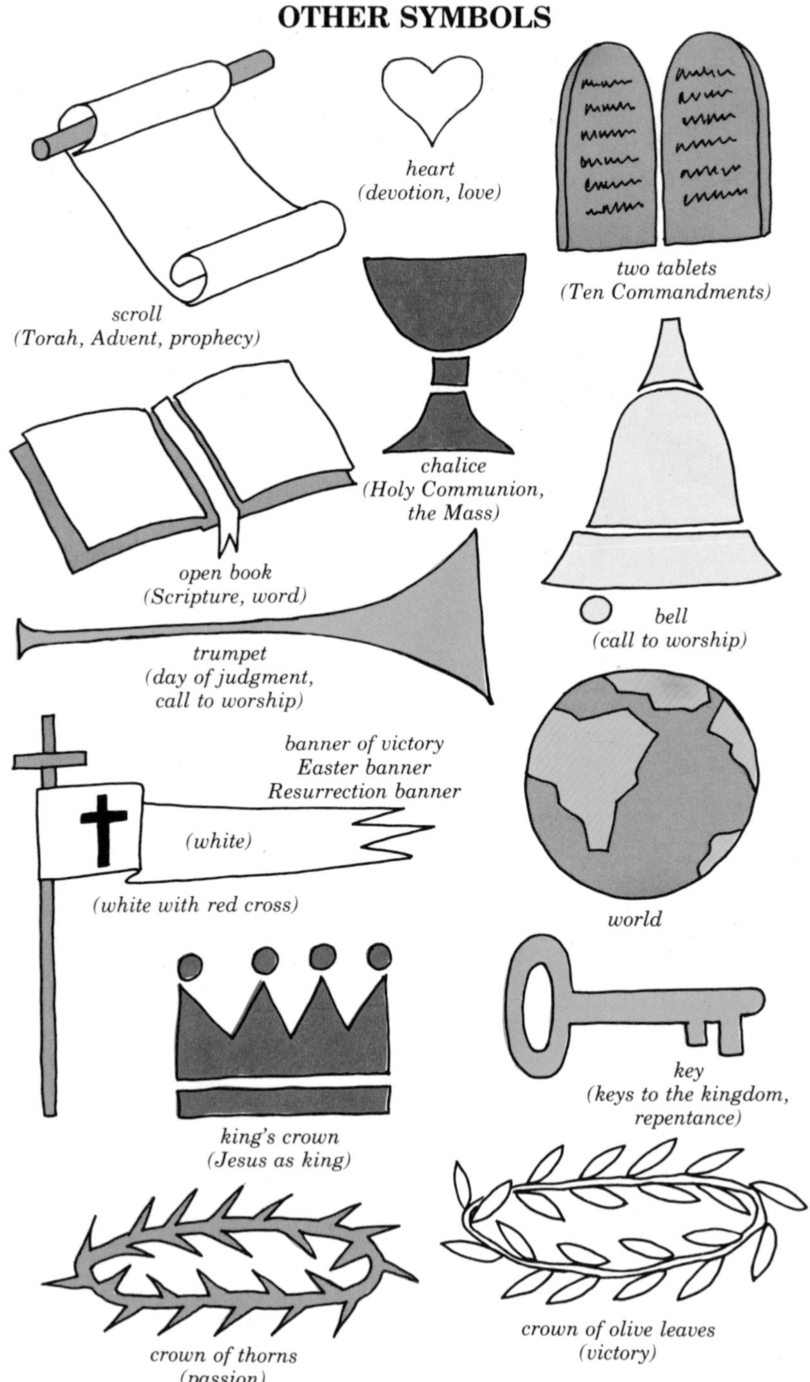

COLOR SYMBOLISM

white
joy, purity, light, holiness, Jesus (Matthew 17:1-2)

green
nature (life), growth, hope

red
blood, love, fire (with zeal, Nahum 2:3)

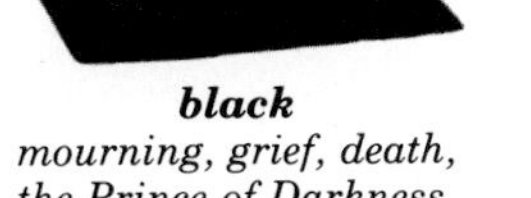

purple or violet
royalty, preparation, suffering, fasting, penitence (John 19:2)

black
mourning, grief, death, the Prince of Darkness.

Other colors often used but not part of the Christian calendar:

gold
in place of or in combination with white

brown
earth, spiritual death, renunciation of the world

blue
heaven, deity (Exodus 28:28-29; 39:30-31; Numbers 15:37-40) Also, traditionally, blue represents the Virgin Mary

gray
humility

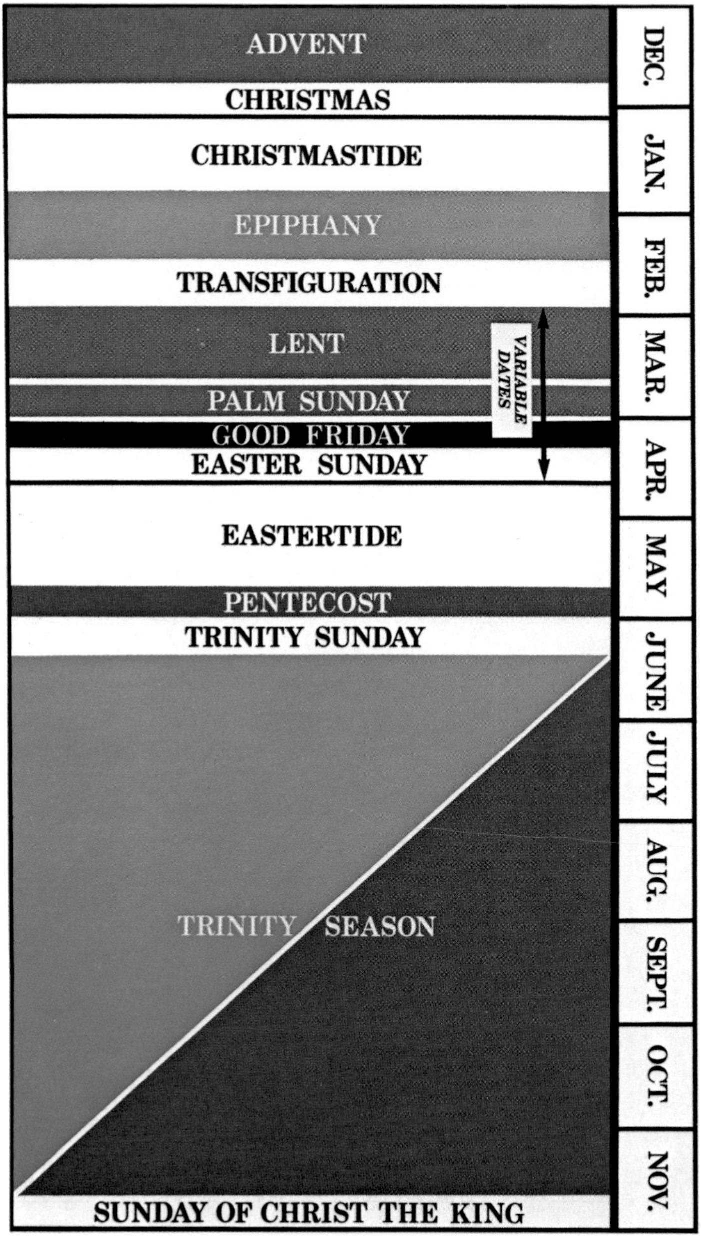

ADVENT

CHRISTMAS

CHRISTMASTIDE

EPIPHANY

TRANSFIGURATION

LENT

PALM SUNDAY

GOOD FRIDAY

EASTER SUNDAY

VARIABLE DATES

EASTERTIDE

PENTECOST

TRINITY SUNDAY

TRINITY SEASON

SUNDAY OF CHRIST THE KING

DEC.

JAN.

FEB.

MAR.

APR.

MAY

JUNE

JULY

AUG.

SEPT.

OCT.

NOV.

This chart is meant to be a general guide to the use of color in the Christian year. Specific information is available on denominational calendars.

Symbolic designs may also be created for the following, plus many other items and concepts:

Altar	*Sword*	*Robe*	*Moon*
Steeple	*Ark*	*Manger*	*Golden Rule*
Throne	*Lion*	*Angels*	*Unity*
Armor	*Raven*	*Earth*	*Friendship*
Coins	*Rose*	*Sea*	*Foot-washing*
Dice	*Thorns*	*Sky*	*Church*
Nails	*Oil*	*Liberty*	*Space*

SACRED MONOGRAMS

Greek spelling of Jesus (Iota Eta Sigma)

(substitutes the Latin "S")

first letter in the Greek spelling of Christ (Chi)

or

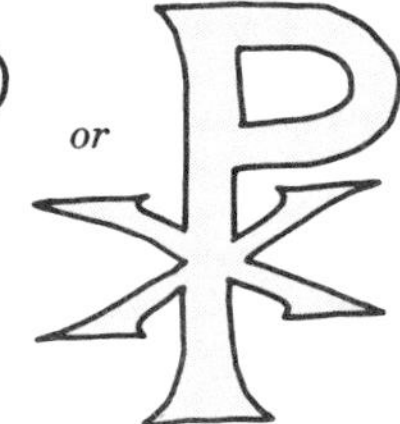

first two letters in the Greek spelling of Christ (Chi Rho)

first and last letters of the Greek alphabet (Alpha Omega) "The beginning and the end"

"Jesus of Nazareth, king of Jews" (used over the cross at the crucifixion)

represents "NIKA," the Greek word for "victor"

ICHTHUS

Greek word for fish (letters stand for "Jesus, Christ, Son of God, Savior. Precious symbol of Christians during the persecution)

COMBINATIONS

Any symbols and monograms may be combined to enhance a message. Below are some examples.

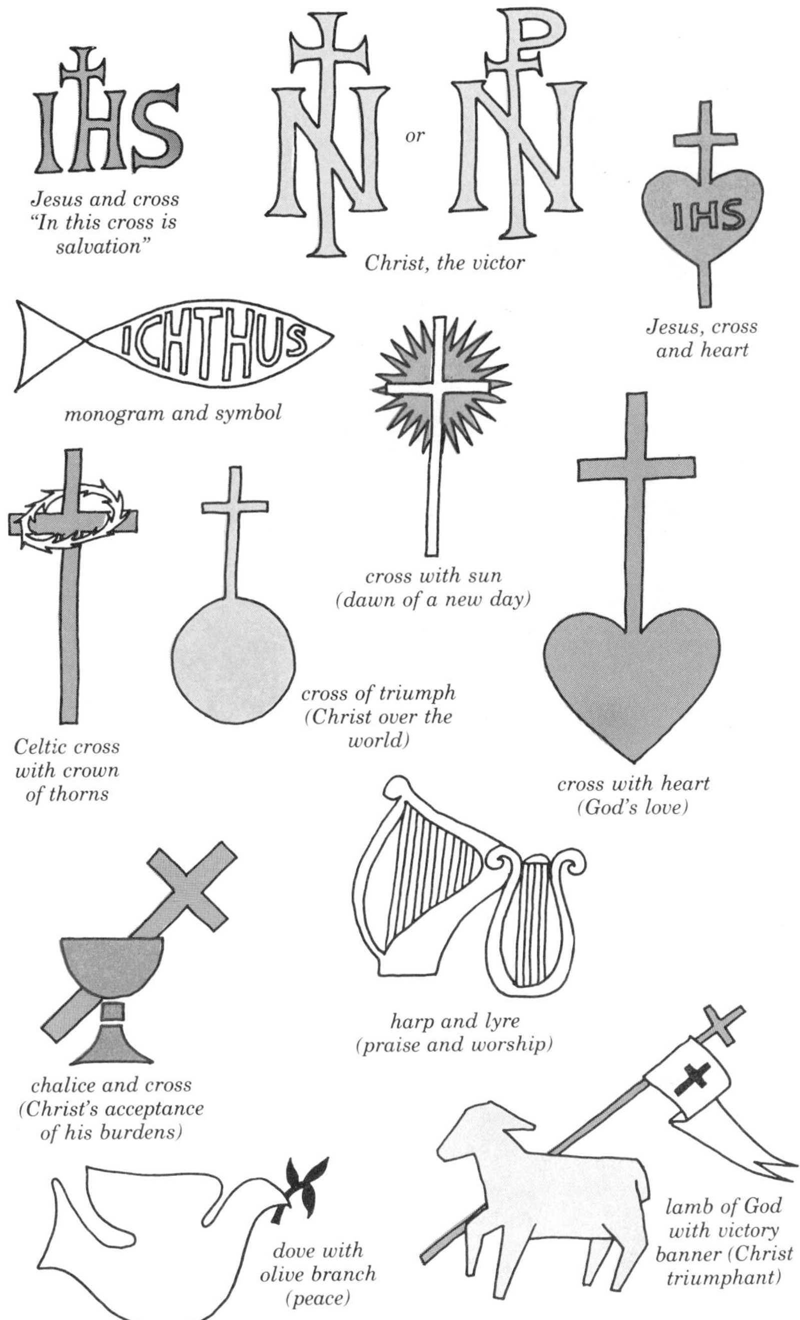

Jesus and cross "In this cross is salvation"

or

Christ, the victor

Jesus, cross and heart

monogram and symbol

cross with sun (dawn of a new day)

Celtic cross with crown of thorns

cross of triumph (Christ over the world)

cross with heart (God's love)

chalice and cross (Christ's acceptance of his burdens)

harp and lyre (praise and worship)

dove with olive branch (peace)

lamb of God with victory banner (Christ triumphant)

THE SHIELDS OF THE APOSTLES

Through the years of mixing legend, fact, and tradition, symbols evolved for each of the twelve apostles. Usually, these symbols appear on shields, signifying faith, protection, bravery, and "soldiers of Christ." The shields could be developed into one large banner to be used as a teaching tool in Bible study. One symbolic shield could be placed on the banner as each apostle is studied. The final product would then become a wall hanging. Or, twelve small banners could be constructed and used in teaching children. These might be mounted on poles and carried in a procession, or, they might be used in a short skit, such as the one that follows. Basic symbols for each apostle are included, though shapes of shields may vary (see Chapter 2, page 18).

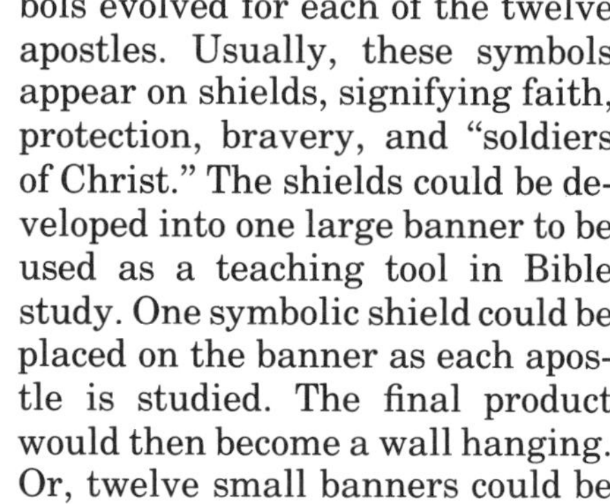

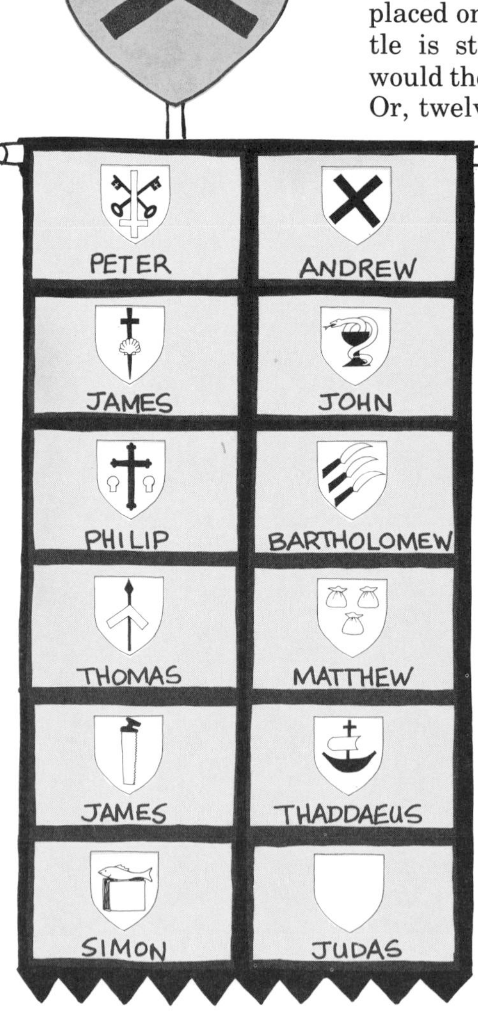

BANNER SKIT FOR CHILDREN

"I Am an Apostle"

NARRATOR:

(Reads Luke 6:12-16) **Tonight we present to you the twelve apostles, each carrying a shield that bears his symbol. Shields were an important part of a soldier's equipment in the time of Christ, and the apostles were very special soldiers. The traditional symbolism on these shields is striking, often tragic and sad, but always inspiring.**

(First Child approaches platform carrying Peter's shield.)

CHILD #1:

My name is Peter. I was a fisherman when Jesus called me to follow him.

NARRATOR:

The keys on Peter's shield represent the "keys to the kingdom of heaven," which Jesus gave to him. The cross upon which Peter was crucified is upside down, because he felt unworthy to die exactly as Jesus did.

CHILD #2:

(Enters with Andrew's shield.) **I am Andrew, brother of Peter. I, too, was a fisherman when Jesus called me.**

NARRATOR:

Andrew died bound to an X-shaped cross. He,

like his brother, chose a cross different from the one used to crucify Jesus. The X cross is called "Saint Andrew's Cross" in memory of this apostle.

CHILD #3:

(Enters, carrying James' shield.) **My name is James and I am the son of Zebedee, also a fisherman.**

NARRATOR:

The scallop shell on James' shield represents his sea journey to Spain as a missionary. The sword refers to his death under the sword of Herod.

CHILD #4:

(Enters, carrying John's shield.) **I, John, am also a fisherman and the son of Zebedee. James is my brother.**

NARRATOR:

According to legend, someone put poison in John's cup, but John realized it and commanded the poison to leave. The serpent represents the poison. The cup also represents another cup — the one that Jesus offered him.

CHILD #5:

(Enters, carrying Philip's shield.) **My name is Philip. I am from Bethsaida on the Sea of Galilee.**

NARRATOR:

Philip's shield contains two loaves of bread, referring to his interest in the feeding of the five thousand. The cross symbolizes his life, his following the way of the cross.

CHILD #6:

(Enters, carrying Bartholomew's shield.) **I am Bartholomew, Philip's friend.**

NARRATOR:

Bartholomew was instrumental in winning Armenia to Christianity. However, his efforts were rewarded by violent death at the hands of angry pagans. The knives on his shield symbolize his martyrdom.

CHILD #7:

(Enters, carrying Thomas' shield.) **My name is Thomas. I had trouble believing, until Jesus taught me a lesson in faith.**

NARRATOR:

According to tradition, Thomas built a church in India with his own hands. That is why the carpenter's square appears on his shield. The spear reminds us of his death at the hands of a pagan priest.

CHILD #8:

(Enters, carrying Matthew's shield.) **My name is Matthew. I was a tax collector when Jesus asked me to follow him.**

NARRATOR:

"And as Jesus passed forth from thence, he saw a man, named Matthew, sitting at the receipt of custom: and he saith unto him, 'Follow me.' And he arose and followed him." The money bags on Matthew's shield refer to his years as a tax collector.

CHILD #9:

(Enters, carrying the shield of James the Less.) **I am James, the son of Alphaeus, also called "James the Less."**

NARRATOR:

James the Less is said to have been the first bishop of Jerusalem. According to tradition, his enemies threw him from the top of the temple when he was ninety-six years old. The saw on his shield refers to the saw used to destroy his body after death.

CHILD #10:

(Enters, carrying Thaddaeus' shield.) **My name is Thaddaeus. Bartholomew and Simon are my friends.**

NARRATOR:

The sailboat on Thaddaeus' shield has a cross for a mast. This symbol reminds us of the missionary journeys of this apostle.

CHILD #11:

(Enters, carrying Simon's shield.) **I am Simon the Zealot. Jesus taught me to add charity and justice to my enthusiasm.**

NARRATOR:

Simon, a "fisher of men," is represented by a fish resting upon a book. The book is the Gospel — the "good news" of Jesus Christ.

CHILD #12:

(Enters, carrying Judas' shield.) **My name is Judas Iscariot. I loved Jesus, but I loved money even more. When I realized my mistake, it was too late.**

NARRATOR:

Judas, because he betrayed Jesus, has no symbol. He is represented by a blank yellow shield.

Song:

(Sung by the twelve children.) "There Were Twelve

Disciples" ***(Children Sing,*** David C. Cook Publishing Co., page 53)

NARRATOR:

All of the twelve were asked to follow Jesus. They followed willingly, not knowing that Jesus would lead them to the cross. Today, everyone who follows Jesus — truly follows Him — will, at sometime in life, bear a cross. Yet Christians do so willingly, finding strength in His strength, joy in His joy, peace in His love.

Closing Song:

(Sung by all.) "I Will Make You Fishers of Men" ***(Sing and Be Happy,*** Word Music, Inc., page 60)

(Children process through congregation, carrying their shield-banners as song is sung. Children then exit with Narrator.)

Chapter 4

Designing Banners

Creativity is an essential part of banner ministry, especially if banners are to express the feelings, stories, ideas, and themes of a particular person or group of people. It is easy to copy someone else's work; it is more difficult (yet more rewarding) to create something new. A challenge. Even if words and symbols from another banner have served as inspiration, they should be put together in a different way, a way that reflects the personalities of those who are presently creating.

Inspiration comes from the environment — nature, places, people, relationships, feelings — and, with the help of scripture, poetry, literature, music (whatever the designer finds interesting) is capsuled into themes. Themes sprout messages.

Explore the environment
Become sensitive
Gather ideas
Choose a theme
Develop a message

The following list of words may be used as thought-starters:

joy	*war*	*peace*
hunger	*love*	*discipleship*
prayer	*praise*	*spirit*
music	*drugs*	*spring*
communion	*humanity*	*poverty*
thanks	*truth*	*life*
faith	*honor*	*service*
friendship	*patience*	*triumph*
trinity	*light*	*death*
hope	*adoration*	*pride*
challenge	*loyalty*	*unity*

Another way to stimulate the thought process is to ask questions:

—*If I could be a child again, what would I say to adults?*

—*What would I really like to tell my best friend? My worst enemy?*

—*What makes me happy? What annoys me?*

—*If I had only one thing to say before dying, what would it be?*

Or, try defining words from the above list:

Hope is . . .

Honor is . . .

. . . is life's greatest challenge.

Next step: Choose symbols, letters, and colors to create the right mood for the message.

Shapes and sizes of letters are endless and are effectively mixed on banners. In general, words to be emphasized are larger and thicker, differently designed, or differently placed.

Once a basic type of letter is selected, improvising can begin. Letters may be:

ROUND SQUARE

THIN UPPER CASE

HEAVY lower case

Angular Script

Freehand

DESIGNER ABSTRACT

TRADITIONAL

Computerized

They may be placed:

Evenly

Angled

VERTICALLY

BOUNCED

IRREGULARLY

OVERLAPPED

as long as they are not

Letter styles show

They may

Letters may be cut out,

painted on,

or made from yarn.

WORD PLACEMENT:

Leave the space of a small "o" between words:

Space like this

Not like this

Words should always be placed close together. They can be:

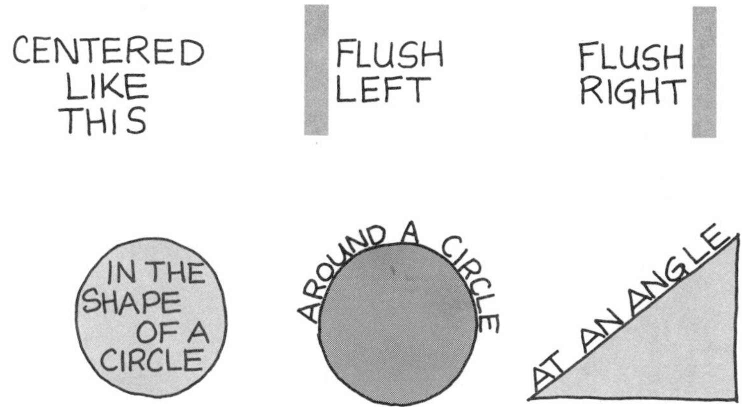

Do **not** place words:

Placement of words is determined by the shape of the banner and the focus of the message. Symbols may be created from geometric shapes.

color helps set mood

In addition to the liturgical symbolic uses of color discussed in chapter 3, color is also used to create mood:

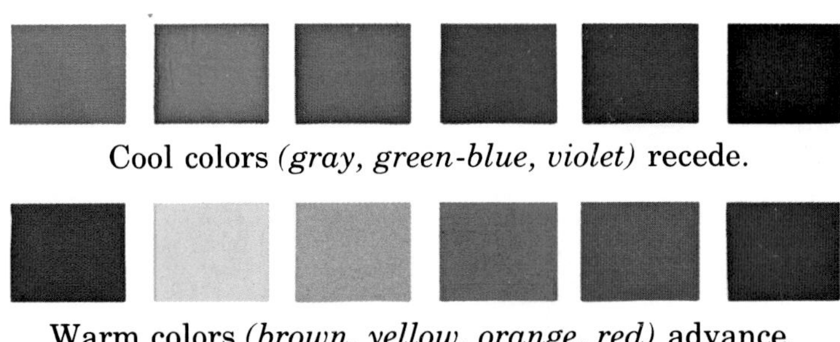

Cool colors *(gray, green-blue, violet)* recede.

Warm colors *(brown, yellow, orange, red)* advance.

Loud colors *(brilliant, florescent)* draw attention.

Soft colors *(pastel)* are subtle.

Cool colors are generally used for backgrounds. In the foreground they project solemnity. Warm colors are joyous and festive and are most effective when used on a cool background.

cool color
warm background

warm color
cool background

THE COLOR WHEEL

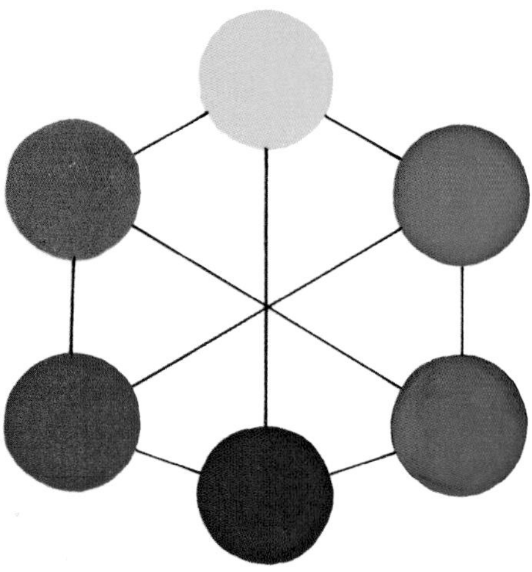

Colors that are next to each other on the wheel (analogous colors) are closely related and blend well. They create a peaceful, pleasing mood when used together. Colors opposite on the wheel are complementary. When used together, their contrast attracts attention. Black and white when used together or in combination with other colors add contrast and heighten the appearance of the other colors.

analogous colors

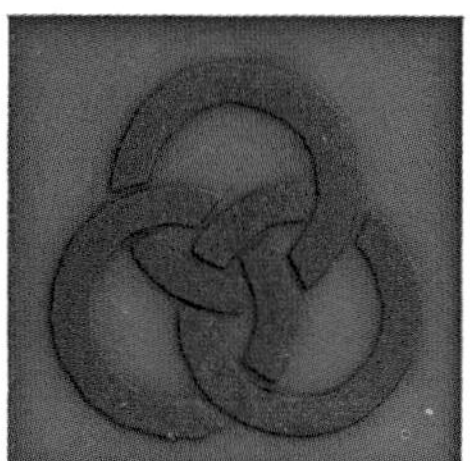

complementary colors

black and white with color

Consider the following concepts when selecting and placing symbols and letters:

DIRECTION

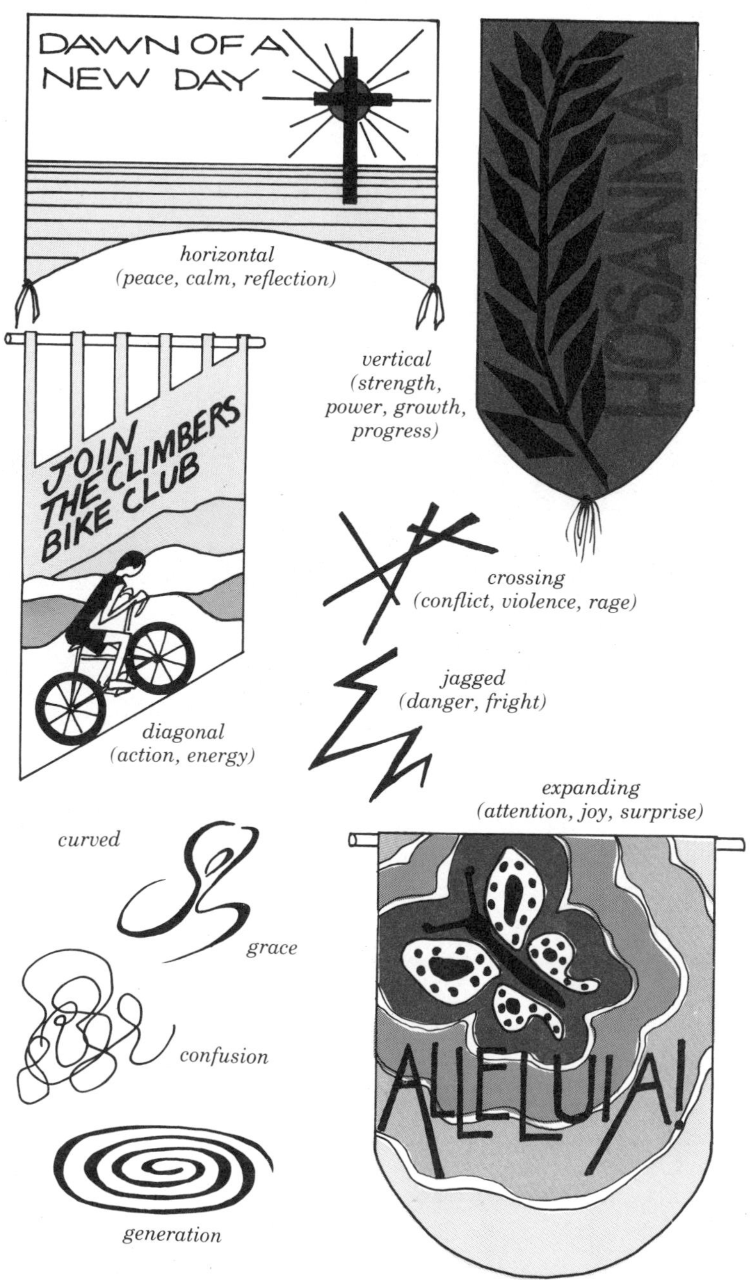

horizontal (peace, calm, reflection)

vertical (strength, power, growth, progress)

diagonal (action, energy)

crossing (conflict, violence, rage)

jagged (danger, fright)

expanding (attention, joy, surprise)

curved

grace

confusion

generation

SHAPE

geometric

3-dimensional

organic

solid

fragmented

positive & negative

BALANCE

formal (static, symmetrical, centered)

informal (dynamic, assymetrical, off center)

contrast

FOCUS

repetition

gradation

too complex

simplified

simplicity

The best way to create your own banner is to experiment. Try different placements of your design on paper by sketching blocks where words or shapes might be placed.

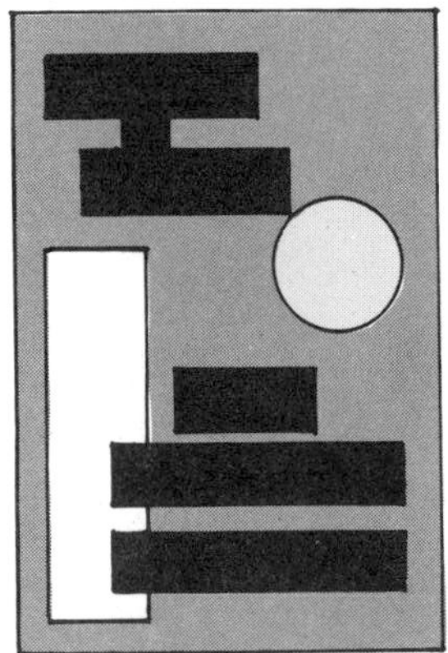

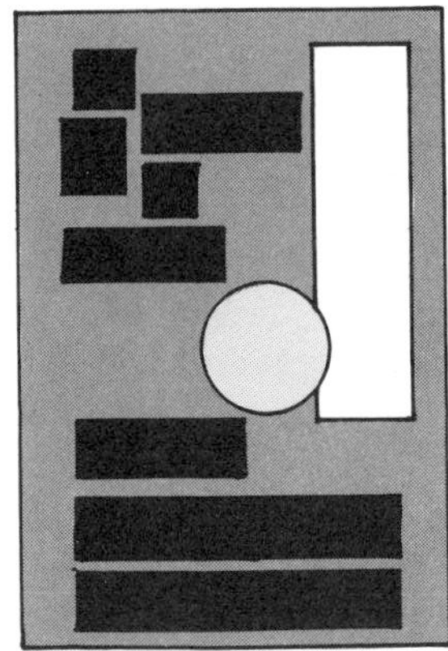

Or, use blocks cut from various colors of construction paper. Arrange and rearrange until not only the placement but also the colors achieve the effect you want. Then make final decisions on lettering style, banner shape, and detail.

Banners, in order to be "blessings," need not be designed by professional artists. Any interested person with a knowledge of basic technique and a "desire to inspire" can create an attractive, meaningful banner.

Chapter 5

Constructing Banners

MAKING PATTERNS

Basic patterns for block letters can be made from strips of paper.

Step 1:

Cut strips of paper the height and length desired for each word.

or

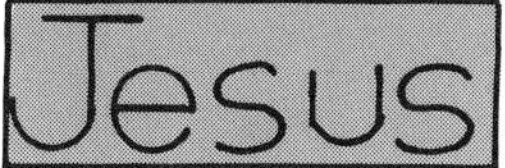

These strips are helpful in planning the lettering layout of the design. Arrange and re-arrange the strips until the placement is pleasing.

Step 2:

Divide each strip into rectangles, one for each letter. Be sure that each rectangle is the right width for its letter. Example: "i" and "l" take less space than "w" or "s".

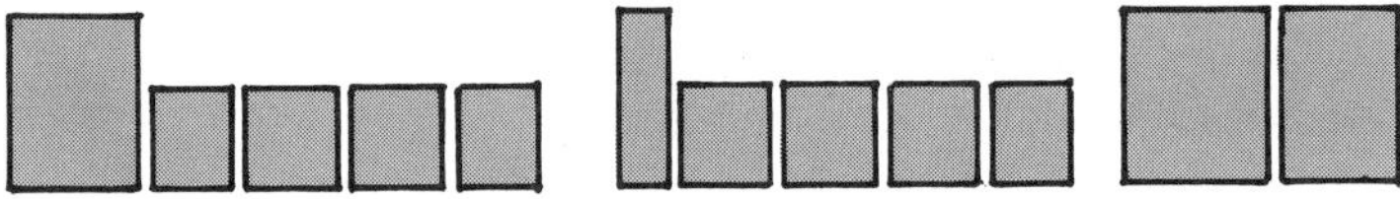

Step 3:

Draw each letter within its rectangle, then cut.

Step 4:

Patterns may be used as they are, or they may be embellished — "played with!"

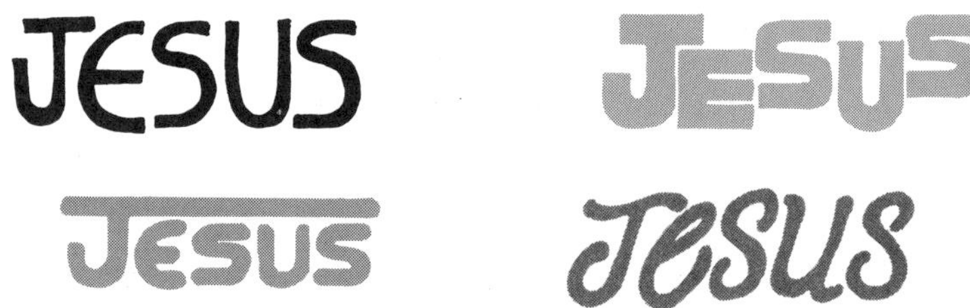

Patterns for symbols may be made from geometric shapes,

or they may be drawn freehand and enlarged. If already large, they may be traced. If symmetrical, they may be cut from a folded piece of paper.

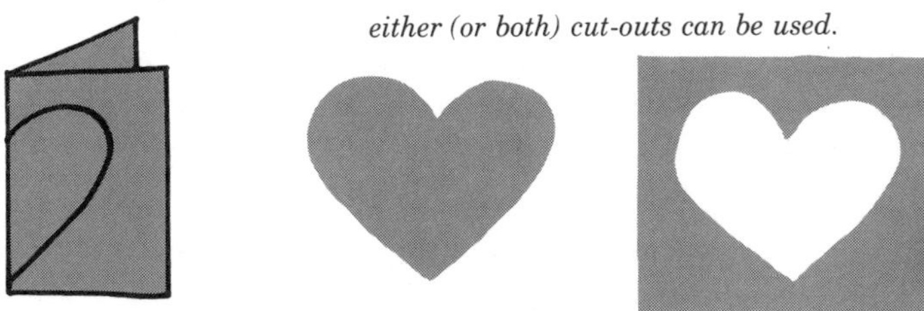
either (or both) cut-outs can be used.

Cut and spread for a different effect.

Once the basic design is settled upon, it is ready to be enlarged onto paper from which the final patterns will be cut.

ENLARGING

Step 1:

Draw evenly spaced grid lines over your design, or do it the easy way — purchase transparent graph paper and tape it over your design! "TransGraph-X" brand is available in craft shops and department stores or from L. J. Originals, Inc., 516 Sumac Place, DeSoto, TX 75115. (Use their heavy black lines for a larger grid.)

If this design were scaled 3 inches per square, the finished design area would be 24"x42".

Using a large sheet of paper (newsprint works nicely), draw grid lines according to the scale chosen. Measure carefully.

Step 2:

Copy your design onto the large (newsprint) grid, which you have just drawn, using the grid lines on your original drawing as a guide.

Step 3:

Label each piece with its color, or mark with corresponding crayons. These newsprint pieces will become the patterns you will use to cut fabric pieces.

CHOOSING MATERIALS

When choosing materials for a banner, consider how the banner will be used. Will it be hung, carried in a procession, moved from room to room? This will determine how durable the banner must be. Perhaps, depending on use, it should even be washable. If the symbols and letters are of heavy material, the background must be substantial enough to support their weight without sagging.

Consider also the texture of materials — rough, smooth, dull, glossy, patterned. Would a combination of textures heighten the effect of the message or detract from it?

Here is a list of recommended materials for background, symbols, and letters:

Felt (inexpensive, doesn't fray, variety of colors, wool or washable 100% acrylic comes in 36" and 72" widths or in 10"x12" squares)

Burlap (inexpensive, supports other fabrics well, can be used for temporary disposable banners, tends to fade and fray, widths to 50")

Textured linen (hangs well, available in a variety of sizes and colors, takes dyes and paints well, washable)

Corduroy, canvas, denim (good weight, variety of colors, washable)

No-wale corduroy, velvet, cotton velveteen (for rich color and texture)

Satin, silk, vinyl, leather, lace, terry cloth, netting, fur, metallic and **brocaded fabrics** (for special texture effects)

Upholstery fabric (gives good support for background)

Muslin or **cotton blends** (used for background lining to give added support)

For one-time use, letters and symbols cut from construction paper may be glued onto cloth. Rubber cement works well for this.

PREPARATION

Step 1:

After colors and fabrics have been determined, the background must be prepared.

a. Cut to desired dimensions, allowing extra material at top and bottom for finishing. If the banner is to be lined, include seam allowance on all sides. **Note:** Some banner makers prefer to line the background material first; others wait to line the finished banner. Many banners are left unlined.
b. Sew a hem at the top, into which a dowel or other hanger can be inserted; or, sew on tabs;

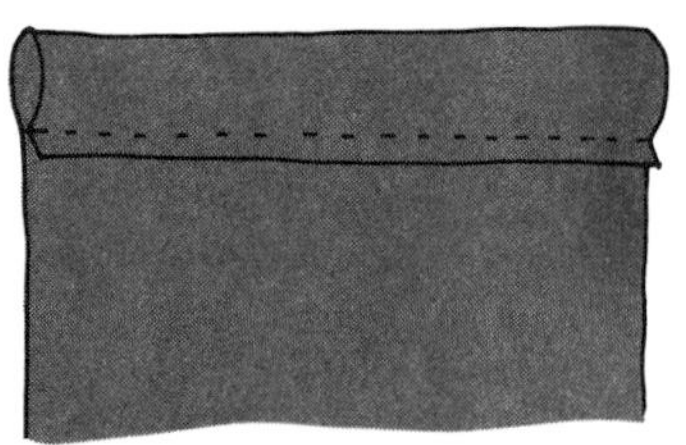

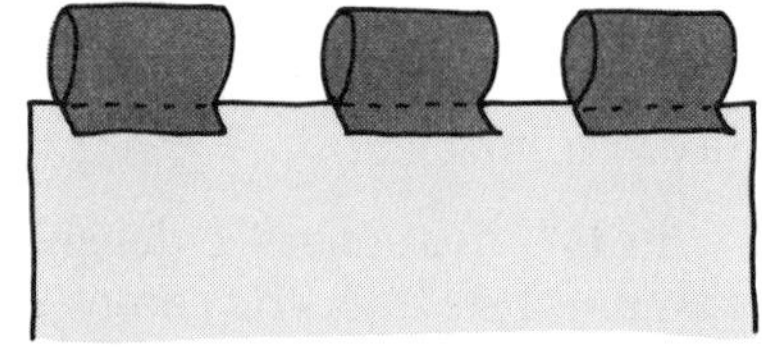

or, cut tabs into top edge, fold, and sew. Also consider using eyelets and cord or yarn, which may be decorated with beads.

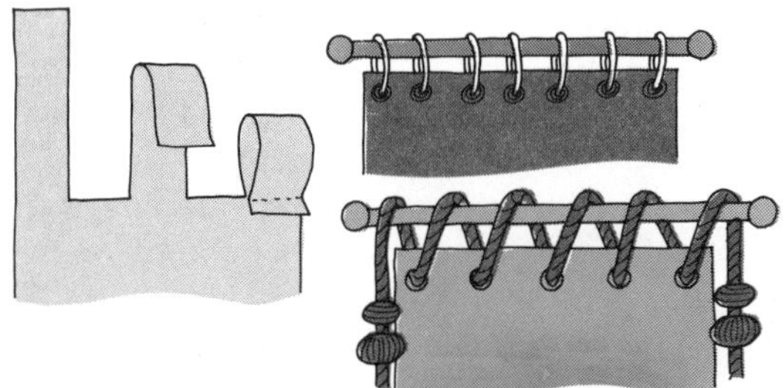

Step 2:

Cut designs from selected materials using the paper patterns already prepared. Use lots of pins so that the patterns don't slip while cutting.

Step 3:

Before attaching designs to the background, assemble any pieces that overlap. (Use glue or sew them.)

ASSEMBLY

Arrange designs on the background. If they are to be glued, cover the back of each design with fabric glue and put in place. Be sure to glue the edges down. If they are to be sewn, use plenty of pins plus a small amount of glue around the edges to prevent slipping. Sewing may be done by hand (hem stitch or embroidery) or by machine (straight stitch or zig-zag). See Chapter 6, "Special Techniques," for further explanation. Designs may also be ironed on by using a product called "Stitch-Witchery," available at fabric stores. This product fuses the fabric without discoloring.

"Painted-on" designs is another option. Draw designs on fabric with chalk or soap, then paint them. Acrylic paint works best. See Chapter 6, "Special Techniques," for batik painting.

FINISHING

Some fabric, such as burlap, can be self-fringed by pulling out cross threads from the bottom until fringe is desired length. Stitch

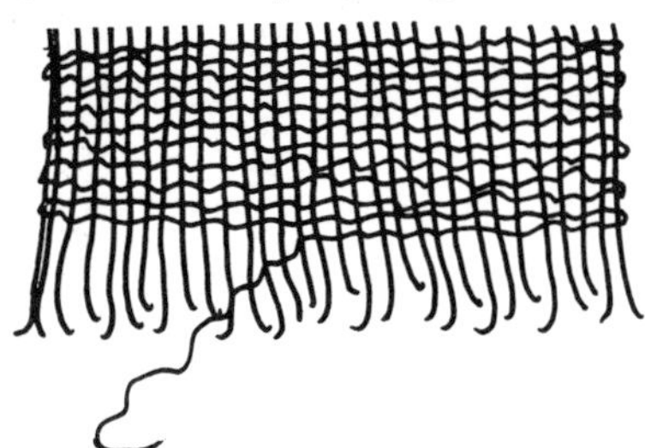

above fringe to keep from fraying.

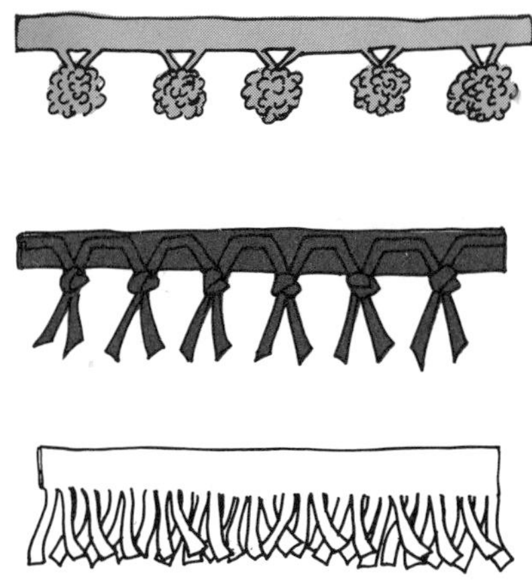

Commercial trimmings may be sewn to the bottom, but homemade ones will make the banner more personal. Consider tassels, pompons, beads, buttons, and macramé knots in addition to fringe. References to fringe date back to Old Testament times.

". . . bid them make fringes in the borders of their garments." *(Numbers 15:38)*

Many banners need no bottom trimming at all. Some fabric banners may need to be weighted at the bottom. Weights are available at fabric stores.

HANGING

Wood dowels (¼" to 1" diameter) make good hangers. So do curtain rods with decorative ends.

Depending on the banner's message, other hangers could be used:

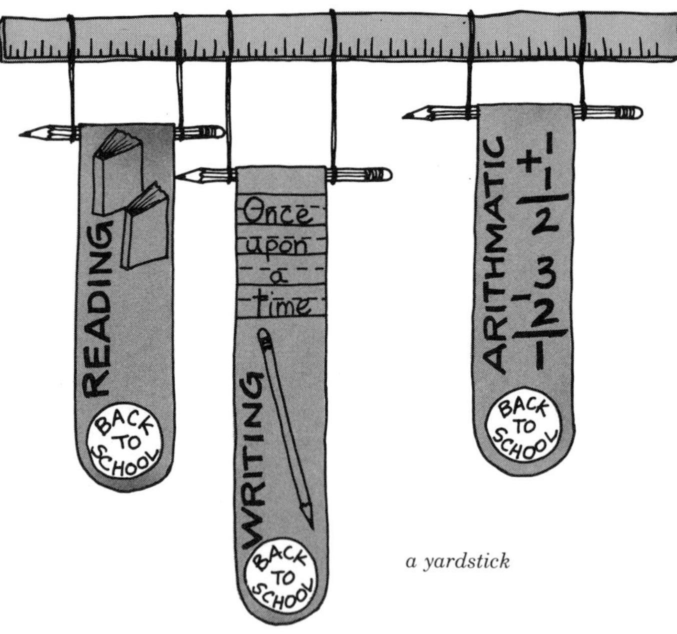

a yardstick

a tennis racket

a tree limb

a lightweight broom

Use the imagination!

MOUNTING AND FRAMING

If a banner has special significance, consider mounting and framing it for preservation and permanence. This not only protects the banner, it also highlights the design and gives it a finished look. Be sure that the framing (with or without glass) does not overpower the banner.

Many lightweight banners, such as computer banners (see Chapter 7), are made more durable and lasting by mounting on posterboard.

DISPLAYING

In addition to vertical hanging and placement on a pole, banners can be displayed in all kinds of creative ways:

hanging horizontally

suspended between poles

flying as a flag

mounted on screens

suspended from the ceiling

Also as a door panel, as a window frame, and (if made of sturdy but temporary material) on the floor.

CHECK-LIST FOR SUPPLIES

1. Paper for patterns, tracing paper
2. Ruler, pencil, chalk or soap, scissors
3. Crayons or markers
4. Background fabric
5. Scraps of material or construction paper for designs
6. Acrylic paint and brushes (optional)
7. Needles, thread, pins
8. Adhesives (fabric glue, rubber cement, Stitch-Witchery)
9. Dowel, rod, or other hanger; decorative ends
10. Rope or cord for hanging
11. Beads, sequins, tassels, pompons, weights (optional)
12. Posterboard, frame (optional)

A machine appliqué banner with machine embroidery and lettering with markers. Designed by Michelle Gallardo.

This banner shows transparent appliqué. The background is felt and the figures are made of netting machine appliquéd in layers. Designed by Michelle Gallardo.

Chapter 6

Special Techniques

APPLIQUÉ AND EMBROIDERY

Appliqué means, simply, one material applied to another. Gluing symbols and letters to a piece of background fabric is a type of appliqué. Sewing, either by hand or by machine, is another.

Any machine stitch is acceptable. Zig-zag is easy to do and holds the edges of the material very well, giving a "finished" looked to the appliqué. Other machine stitches, such as the fish () or the crescent (), may be chosen to blend or contrast with the design.

Appliqué may also be attached by hand using invisible hem stitches or fancy embroidery stitches. Embroidery floss, crewel yarn, metallic thread, and even string may be used, either of contrasting, blending, or like colors.

Try:

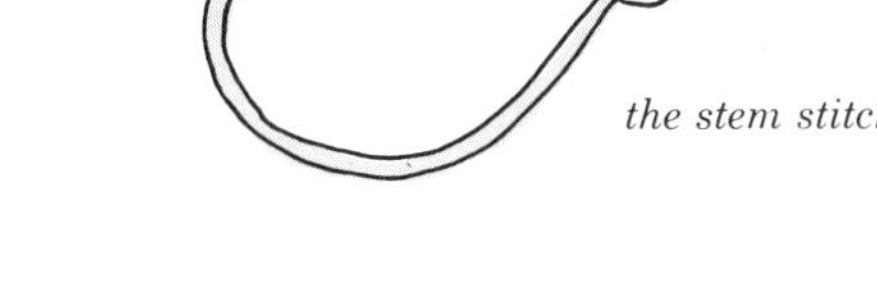

the stem stitch

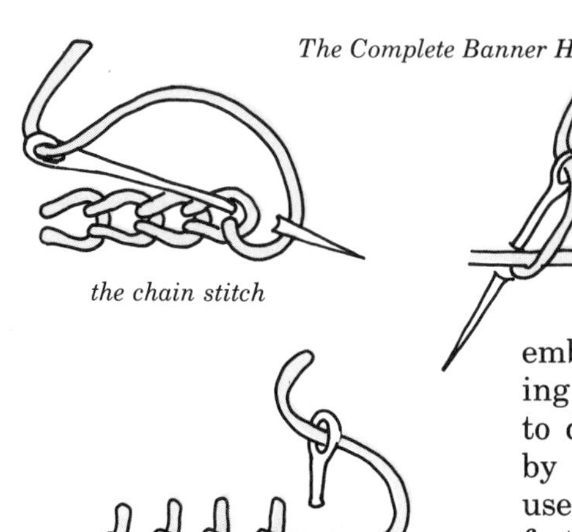

These stitches (and other embroidery stitches, including crewel work) may be used to develop a banner entirely by embroidery, without the use of appliqué. A similar effect could be achieved by gluing yarn or metallic trimming or braid to the background fabric.

STUFFING

Stuffing an appliqué gives a three-dimensional look. Simply slit the background fabric behind the form to be stuffed and fill with cotton or very soft material such as clean, discarded hosiery.

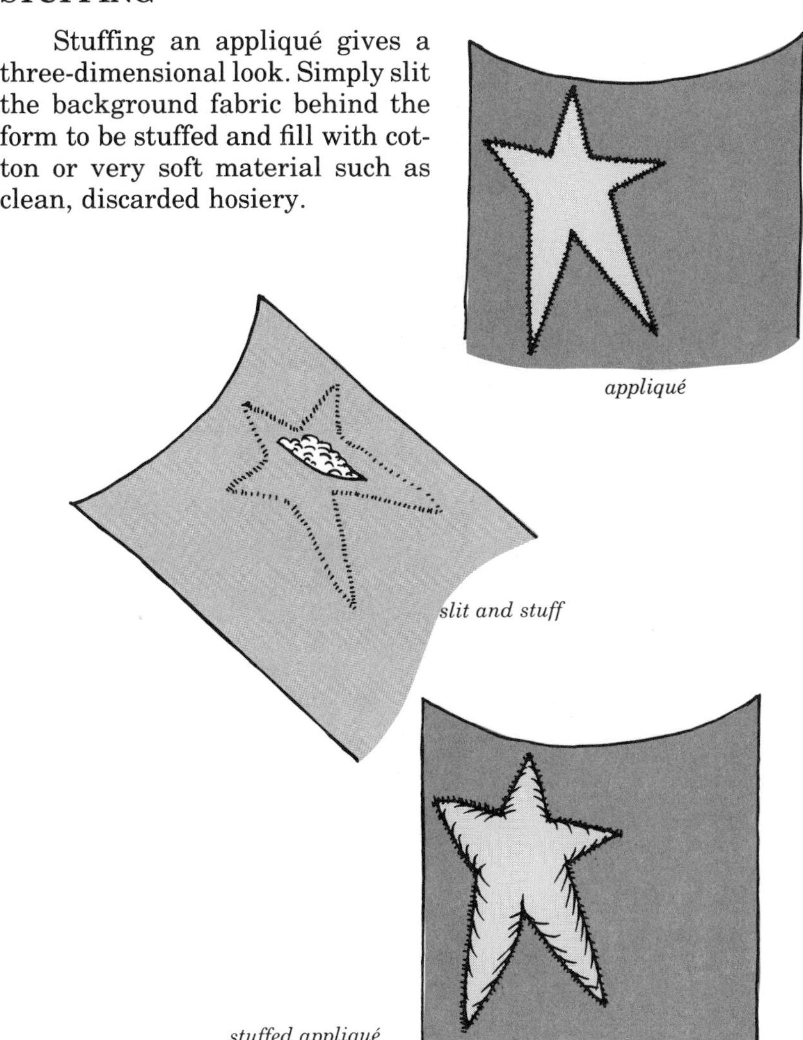

appliqué

slit and stuff

stuffed appliqué

The "For God So Loved the World" banner on the following page was designed and constructed by the banner committee of First United Methodist Church, Loudon, Tennessee. This group has been actively making banners since 1979, when Mrs. W. G. (Faye) House made the first banner as a Christmas offering. Ruth Swenson is the current chairman. Other members are Louise Zimmerman, Lallie Burnette, and Wil and Kay Comstock.

The entire banner is machine-appliquéd. For added dimension the hands could be stuffed and the IHS hand-embroidered on the black cross. Letters could be glued rather than stitched.

TRANSPARENT APPLIQUÉ

For a very different illusive effect, cut symbols from various colors of netting, then appliqué them to the background fabric, allowing the colors to overlap. This works best on a white or light colored fabric. *(See color photo on page 66.)*

BATIK

Batik is an ancient method of fabric design using wax and dyes. The fabric is painted with wax, then cooled and crushed, then dyed. The dye resists the wax and only "takes" on the unpainted portions, leaving a crackled effect. A banner may be waxed and dyed several times in several colors to create complicated designs or to produce simple "layering."

Method: Choose a light colored natural fabric such as cotton, linen, or silk; cut it 4" larger on all sides to allow for shrinkage and finishing; wash and iron it.

Working out of doors, stretch and tack the material to a wooden surface (perhaps a picnic table), which has been covered with paper for protection. Transfer the design onto the fabric using dressmaker's carbon and wheel, or draw it freehand.

Paint the areas to be "saved" with hot wax (a 50-50 mixture of beeswax and paraffin). Wax can be melted on a hot plate, using a double boiler. **Note:** This mixture is highly flammable. Do not work over an open flame!

Beginning with the lightest-colored dye (prepare commercial fabric dye according to package directions), dip the fabric until it attains the desired shade. Be sure to use rubber gloves!

Return the fabric to the covered wooden surface and repeat the process (draw design, paint with wax, dip in dye) until just before the last dye bath.

Now crush the banner in your hands to crack the wax. Dip in last dye bath. Hang on line to dry.

When dry, iron the banner between paper towels to remove the wax. Finish the edges, then dry clean if desired.

TIE-DYEING

Tie-dyeing means that the material is tied in knots or banded, then dipped in dye. The effect is an uneven absorption of dye, which can be controlled by the placement of the ties. Material can be tie-dyed, then re-tied and dyed again with eye-catching results.

One popular tie-dye pattern is called "Sunburst." It is created by holding the material in the middle and banding it several times down its length with string or rubber bands. The tied material is then dipped in dye. When dry, the ties are removed and the material is ironed. Tie-dyed material can be used by itself or as a background for symbols and letters.

Choose a light colored natural fabric and cut it 4" larger on all sides to allow for shrinkage and finishing. Use commercial fabric dye according to package directions.

1. Tie it.
2. Dampen it.
3. Dye it.
4. Dry it.
5. Iron it.
6. Finish it.
7. Use it!

Other popular tie methods are:

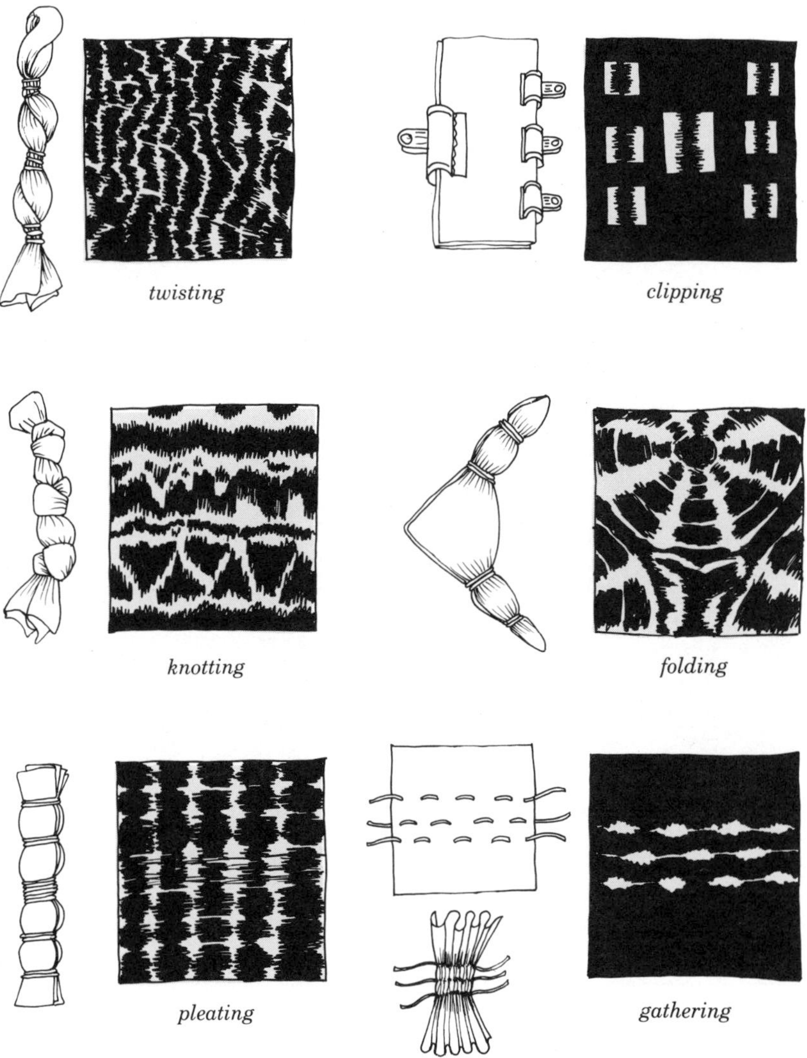

twisting *clipping*

knotting *folding*

pleating *gathering*

Experiment with various ties and dyes to create exciting designs. Tie-dyed material may be washed.

Chapter 7

Computer Banners

Banner-makers nowadays do not necessarily need to be handy with brushes, paint, needles, thread, scissors, or glue. The age of technology is such that a person can have fun with a computer (other than video games!) and be creative, as well as reap its practical benefits. Most computer use in churches so far has been for membership rolls, finance, Christian education, church library, etc. But the computer can also be a tool for involving people who might not otherwise take part in creative church activities.

Computer banners are showing up in schools, churches, and at parties, designed by computer lovers of all ages. They are fragile, but they can, with care, last long enough to be enjoyed by many people.

Some are long strip messages,

some are small paper sheets laced together,

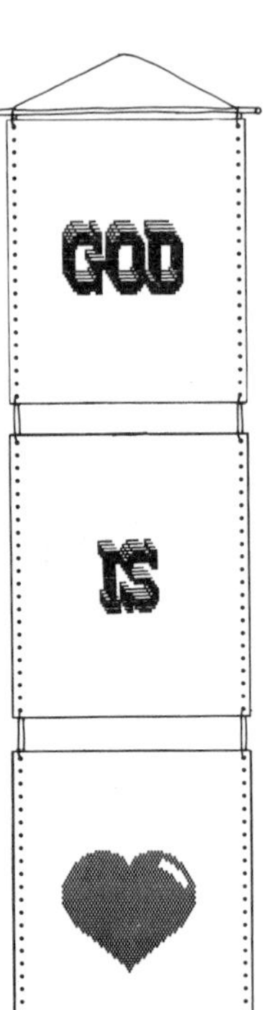

some are temporary wall hangings,

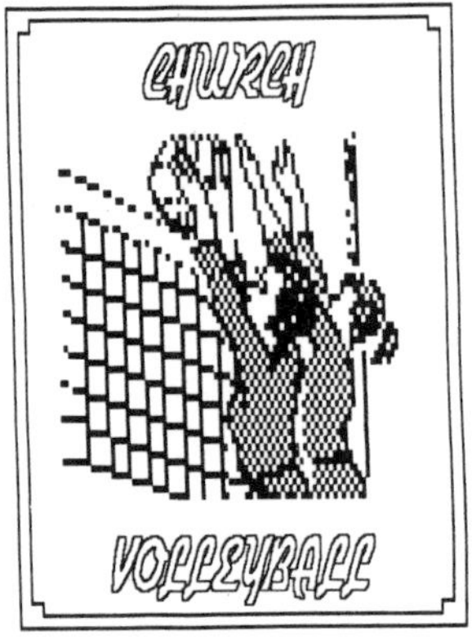

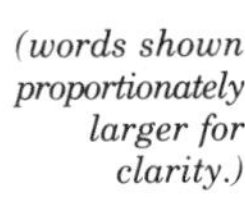
(words shown proportionately larger for clarity.)

and some are elaborately mounted designs.

This design, enhanced with colored pencils, is mounted on blue posterboard. Holes are punched across the bottom, and a thin fringe is made by tying long pieces of string into each hole. Beads are knotted into the string.

The strip banner above ("His banner over me is love") was made on a Radio Shack TRS-80 Model 4P personal computer with a daisy wheel printer (a dot matrix works just as well) and a home-written program. It is hung as is, using some of the holes in the computer paper to tack the strip to the wall.

Each letter is made up of its own smaller letters:

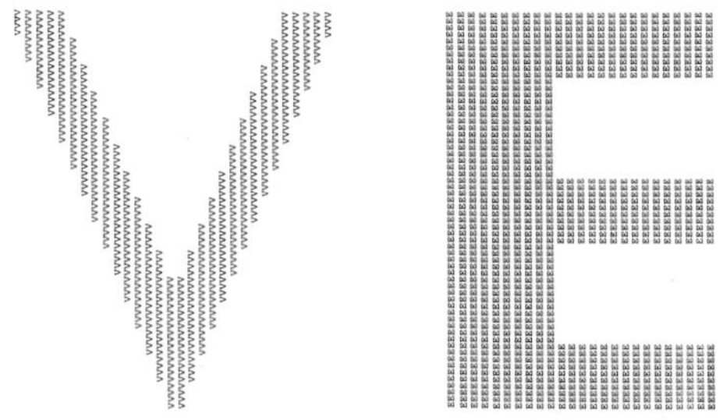

This makes some letters appear to be a lighter shade of print than others, an interesting effect. The same strip produced on another computer, using a different program, might be made of solid letters or letters composed of different design images.

The three banners on page 76 were designed by students at Thomasville High School in Thomasville, Georgia, under the guidance of Mrs. Cheryl Greene. They used an Apple IIe computer. The printer is an Apple DMP, IMAGEWRITER, Scribe. Graphics were created using The Print Shop, © 1984, Broderbund Software.

Using the same computer, printer, and software package, the following banners were designed by Mark Litherland, a student at Georgia Institute of Technology in Atlanta, Georgia.

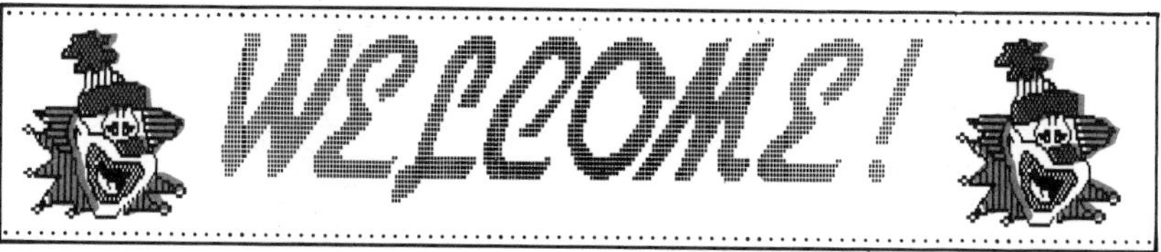

(clowns may be enhanced with colored pencils)

(mounted on a circle of yellow posterboard)

(hung with a Christmas garland)

(stapled to a twist of red, white, and blue crepe paper)
(words shown proportionally larger for clarity)

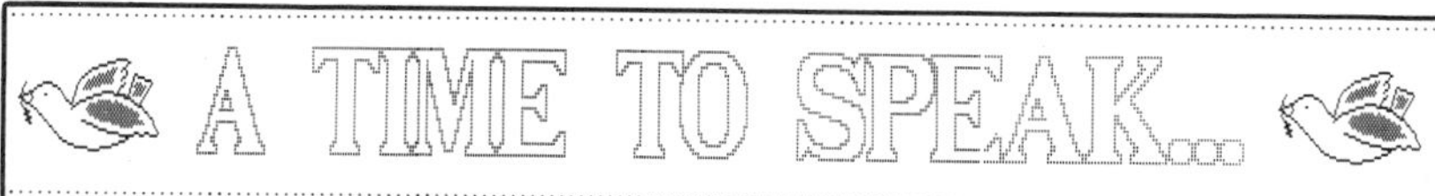

Banners may also be designed from "scratch" by using the graphic editor function of "The Print Shop" software named on the preceding page.

It is possible to print six or eight designs to a page. They may then be cut apart, mounted on colorful posterboard, and used as tree ornaments or parts of a mobile. As a children's activity, pages could be printed in advance and given to the children for coloring, cutting, and assembly.

The following two strip banners were designed by Gene Richardson of Thomasville, Georgia, using the IBM version of "The Print Shop" Broderbund software. The computer is an AT&T 6300 and the printer is an Okidata U93 Microline.

The possibilities in computer banners are endless, and the fun is certainly a unique kind. Find "computer buffs" who are willing to share their skills and/or computers to teach others and to become, themselves, "banner buffs."

Go with the flow — use high technology to

STRETCH

the imagination!

These fruit of the spirit banners were designed for use during the Christmas season, but they can also be used throughout the year. Designed by Anne Kircher.

A visual and liturgical banner titled **The Christmas Banner** *is designed for use during the four weeks of Advent. The design is by Michelle Gallardo and script by Arthur Lewis. The bannerkit includes designs, patterns and a narrative script for up to six layperson speakers. It is available from Contemporary Drama Service.*

Chapter 8

Ideas Plus

I. ABC CHRISTMAS BANNERS

ABC Christmas Banners can be worked into or around a program for children. Children make their own banners in the weeks prior to use. Or, instead of a program, the banners may be hung for the entire congregation's enjoyment during the Christmas season, perhaps along the walls of the Sunday School building or around a fellowship room.

If there are enough children, each one is assigned a letter; or, one child may have two letters on his banner. If there is an abundance of children, two or more may be assigned to one banner.

Alphabet Suggestions

A — Angels
B — Baby, Bethlehem
C — Candles, Carolers
D — Decorations
E — Evergreen
F — Food, Family, Friendship
G — Greetings, Gifts
H — Happiness, Holly, Home
I — Ice, Ivy
J — Jingle Bells, Joseph, Joy

K — Kris Kringle
L — Love
M — Music, Mary, Messiah
N — Neighbors
O — Old-fashioned, O Come All Ye Faithful
P — Peace, Prayer, Partridge in a Pear Tree
Q — Quiet (Silent Night)
R — Reindeer
S — Star, Shepherds, Snowman
T — Tree
U — Universe United (Joy to the World)
V — Vacation
W — Wise men
X — Christ (the Greek "Chi")
Y — Yule Logs
Z — Zest, Zeal

Examples:

II. SCRIPTURE BANNERS

Design a banner based on Galatians 5:22-23, the nine "fruits of the Spirit." Select a symbol for each "fruit" and construct nine small banners. Hang them on an actual tree branch. If it is winter, treat the branch with Christmas snow (aerosol) — fruits of the Spirit bloom all year round! Suspend the branch from the ceiling or stand it upright and secure it in a heavy, dirt-filled pot.

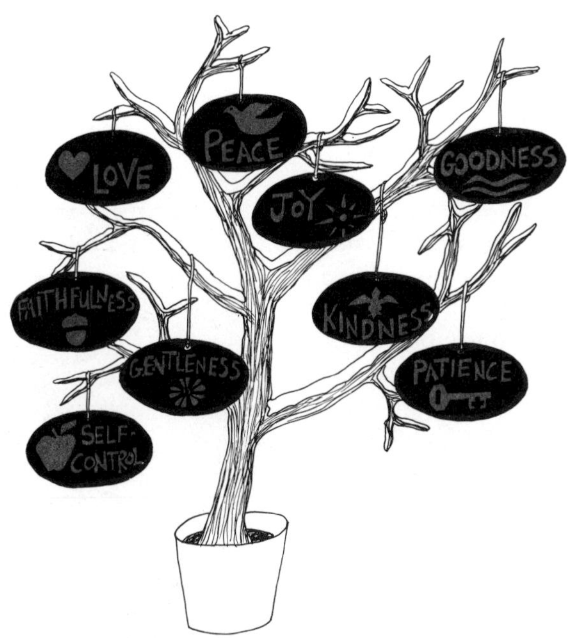

Choose other scriptures and other hanging techniques. Suggestions:

"Behold, I make all things new." *(Revelation 21:5)*

"Look to the rock from whence you are hewn." *(Isaiah 51:1)*

"Make a joyful noise!" *(Psalms 66:1)*

"The time of the singing of birds is come." *(Song of Solomon 2:12)*

"He hath made everything beautiful in his time." *(Ecclesiastes 3:11)*

"Ye have compassed this mountain long enough: turn you northward." *(Deuteronomy 2:3)*

"He who wavers is like a wave of the sea driven with the wind and tossed." *(James 1:6)*

"Study to show thyself approved unto God." *(Timothy 2:3)*

"Love one another as I have loved you." *(John 15:12)*

"Blessed are the peacemakers, for they shall be called the children of God." *(Matthew 5:9)*

III. MUSIC BANNERS

Design music banners, using hymns for themes. Mini-services, with prayer and scripture, can then be developed incorporating the banners. These banners may be temporary one-time-use banners, or permanent banners.

Example: Begin with a plain "sing praise" banner. Using the hymn, "All Things Bright and Beautiful," make appropriate symbols —flower, bird, mountain, river, sun, fruit. Prepare the banner and the symbols with Velcro. Have two or more children attach the symbols as the hymn is sung by the congregation. Scripture reading — Genesis 1:31.

Or: Make three banners, one for each verse of "Fairest Lord Jesus." Attach all three to a standard so that they may be flipped as each verse is sung by the congregation.

Or: Have the choir sing an arrangement of "Fairest Lord Jesus" with all three banners hanging in full view of the congregation.

Other hymns filled with symbolism:

O Worship the King
For the Beauty of the Earth
This Is My Father's World
Joyful, Joyful, We Adore Thee
God of Our Fathers
Crown Him with Many Crowns

Savior, Like a Shepherd Lead Us
Awake, Awake to Love and Work
In Christ There Is No East or West
When the Storms of Life Are Raging, Stand by Me
Lead Kindly Light
We Are Climbing Jacob's Ladder
Battle Hymn of the Republic
America the Beautiful
There's a Song in the Air
Brighten the Corner Where You Are

IV. CHORAL READING BANNERS

Design banners to accompany choral readings. Example: Have a group read, chorally, Psalm 23, "The Lord Is My Shepherd," as a "shepherd" banner is presented to the congregation. This could also be done with inspirational poetry and used as a supplement or a devotional for women's meetings. Consider a "garden" banner and a reading of this whimsical poem by Lucille Cargile Bennett, inspired by Genesis 2:8.

I love the garden you've lent me, Lord
Even the hoein' and weedin'
But I do have one question, Lord
Did you have this trouble in Eden?

I enjoy the work in our garden, Lord
Even the sprayin' it is needin'
But I have been wondering lately, Lord
Did you have any pests in Eden?

I like to rest from my labors, Lord
Especially after re-seedin'
Did you enjoy relaxing, Lord
At the end of the day in Eden?

(used with permission)

Tiny banners focusing on a theme could also be mounted on standards (Popsicle sticks on a wood base) and used as favors or place markers at a banquet.

V. FAMILY BANNERS

Try developing family banners:

VI. GROUP BANNERS

Design a banner to represent your group. Make it a group project.

VII. SPECIAL-USE BANNERS

(Designed by Bob Dixon, artist and Diaconal Minister of Education, The United Methodist Church.)

Suggestion: Edges of blocks in bright colors; contrasting letters on blocks; red, blue, yellow balloons; light brown bear; pink background; yarn strings.

Suggestion: Bright blue background with yellow letters; white hand; center person cut out so that background shows through.

Sometimes the most meaningful banners are those created at random. An example is a banner carried by The Wesley Bell Ringers of Christ United Methodist Church, Salt Lake City, Utah. As the Ringers tour the United States, they collect patches from cities, events, churches, and other groups along their route. Their director, Ed Duncan, sends word ahead so that places they visit are prepared to participate with "store bought" patches, sports patches, high school patches, or homemade patches. This is a "sew as you go" banner, which the entire congregation enjoys when the Ringers return to tell of their travels. The Wesley Bell Ringers have been in existence since 1963. Over the years, more

Wesley Bell Ringers Travel Banner

Wesley Bell Ringers Membership Banner

than 200 Ringers have taken part in 20 summer tours. Another of their banners in progress is the Membership Banner, begun in 1972 by Janet Glodowski. Each Ringer provided a six-inch piece of cloth and symbolically pinned it to a large banner, showing that though each member remains an individual, all are members of the larger organization. After that ceremonial "pinning-on," each piece of cloth was cut into a Cross Crosslet and sewed to the banner. All former ringers were contacted and asked for a scrap of material. The banner was first used at a choir birthday party — still the traditional occasion for the once-a-year pinning of material.

VIII. ODDS 'N ENDS BANNERS

THEATRE IN
THE PARK

BORN
FREE

REVIVAL
BEGINS
WITH
ME!

IX. "THINK ON THESE THINGS"

Nothing Is Impossible
Beacon of Strength
Kiss Frogs
Vital Signs: Caring and Sharing
Happy Birthday, Jesus!
Love Is the Perfect Gift
Between Two Thieves
There's Room in Our Inn!
Renew Your Strength
We All Have Ups and Downs
Get Real!
Plant Seeds of Peace
The Power and the Glory
Hang on for Dear Life!
Live One Life — Live It in the Open
Practice Forgiveness
We Have Seen His Star
Let My People Go
Love Never Gives Up
Do You Like Yourself?
You Can Make a Difference
Because We Believe . . .
Maranatha!
Joy Is Born
Prepare for Liftoff — Salvation Is a Real Trip!
Jesus Is My Song
"Who gives himself with his alms feeds three, Himself, his hungering neighbor, and me" *(Lowell)*

Consider, select, create, construct, and above all enjoy, not only the finished banner but the entire process of bringing it to life.

May all your banners be banners of blessing!

BIBLIOGRAPHY

Broderick, Virginia and Judi Bartholomew. *How to Create Banners.* Northport, NY: Costello Publishing Company, Inc., Franciscan Herald Press, 1977.

Collier's Encyclopedia. NY: Macmillan Educational Corporation, 1979. Vols. 10, 12.

Compton's Encyclopedia. Chicago: F. E. Compton Company, 1975, Vol. 9.

Daves, Michael. *Young Readers Book of Christian Symbolism.* Nashville: Abingdon Press, 1967.

Hall, Warner L. *Symbols of Faith.* Richmond, VA: The Covenant Life Curriculum, The CLC Press. © 1965, Marshall C. Denty.

Kannick, Prebin. *The Flag Book.* NY: M. Barrows & Company, Inc., 1957.

Lauckner, Edie. *Signs of Celebration.* St. Louis: Concordia Publishing House, 1978.

Merit Students Encyclopedia. Bernard S. Cayne, Editor-in-Chief. Crowell-Collier Educational Corporation, 1968.

Ortegel, Sister Adelaide. *Banners and Such.* West Lafayette, IN: The Center for Contemporary Celebration, 1971.

Rainey, Sarita R. *Wall Hangings: Designing with Fabric and Thread.* Worcester, MA: Davis Publications, Inc., 1971.

Rest, Friedrich. *Our Christian Symbols.* Philadelphia: The Christian Education Press, 1954.

Smith, Whitney. *Flags Through the Ages and Across the World.* NY: McGraw-Hill Book Company, 1975.

Stafford, Thomas Albert. *Christian Symbolism in the Evangelical Churches.* Nashville: Abingdon-Cokesbury Press, MCMXLII.

Wetzler, Robert P. and Helen Huntington. *Seasons & Symbols.* Minneapolis: Augsburg Publishing House, 1962.

Wolfe, Betty. *The Banner Book.* Wilton, CT: Morehouse-Barlow Co., Inc., 1974.

ABOUT THE AUTHOR

Janet Litherland is a professional writer from the southeastern United States. She began her career by working as an actress doing stock, off-Broadway, road shows and an overseas tour for USO. She uniquely joined her interests and training in the arts after meeting, and later marrying, Jerry Litherland. Jerry was on his way to study at a seminary, and when he was able to have his own parish, Janet had at her hands a training ground for religious drama work during the 10 years her husband was a minister. Janet has directed drama groups for churches and schools and is currently a director of music in a United Methodist church. She and Jerry are the parents of two teenaged sons, Mark and Steve.

Janet has been published in several national magazines. She has written religious drama materials for Baker's Plays, Lillenas Publishing Company and Contemporary Drama Service. Her large body of work for the latter includes several resource kits on clown ministry, including "The Clown as Minister I and II" and "Scripture Skits for a Troupe of Clowns;" "The Wonderful Art of Storytelling," a resource kit for storytellers; and "Five Women, Beautiful Within," a set of monologs for women. She is also the author of *Youth Ministry from Start to Finish* and of the best-selling book, *The Clown Ministry Handbook,* published by Meriwether Publishing Ltd.

Janet's accomplishments in playwriting include first-place awards from the Georgia Theatre Conference Playwriting Competition and the Philadelphia, Pennsylvania, Writers' Conference. Her education in theatre arts and music was obtained through work at Indiana University of Pennsylvania and the Musical Theatre Academy of New York City.

More banner ideas from Contemporary Drama Service:

The Thanksgiving Banner
A banner worship service for the Thanksgiving season

The Children's Christmas Banners
Two banners which portray the main events of Christmas together with a scripted presentation

The Children's Advent Banners

Four symbolic banners which portray the main events of Advent together with a scripted presentation

The Advent Banner

Used as a visual and dramatic presentation for Advent

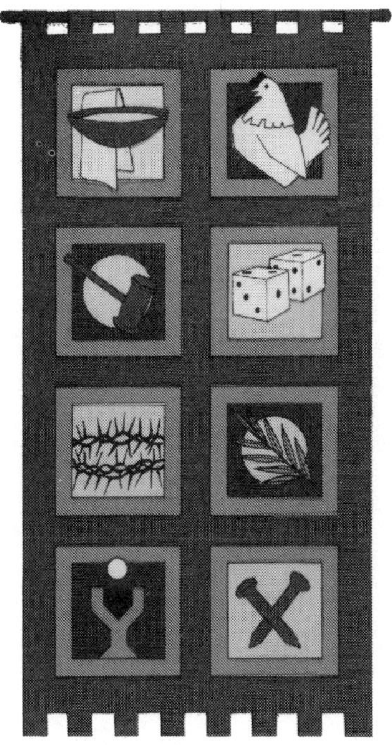

The Lenten Banner

Used as a visual together with a scripted presentation portraying the last days of the life of Jesus

The "I Am the Way" Banner
A banner design symbolizing the theme: Christ, the Eternal

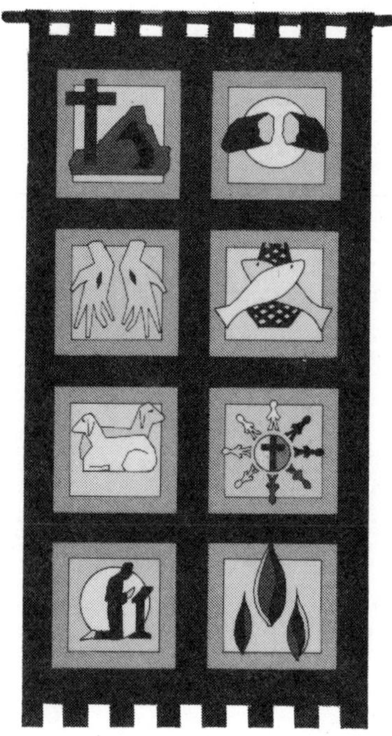

The Great Fifty Days Banner
Used as a visual together with a scripted presentation portraying the events from Easter to Pentecost

"Christ, the Light of the World" Banner
A banner design portraying the theme of Tenebrae

The "He Is Risen" Banner
A banner design symbolizing the resurrection of Christ

For more information about how these and other bannerkits may be ordered send for a free catalog:

Contemporary Drama Service
P.O. Box 7710
Colorado Springs, CO 80933
Telephone: (303)594-4422

ORDER FORM

MERIWETHER PUBLISHING LTD.
P.O. BOX 7710
COLORADO SPRINGS, CO 80933
TELEPHONE: (303)594-4422

Please send me the following books:

_______**The Complete Banner Handbook** **$10.95**
by Janet Litherland #DD-B172
A complete guide to banner design and construction

_______**The Official Sunday School Teachers Handbook #DD-B152** **$7.95**
by Joanne Owens
An indispensable aid and barrel of laughs for anyone involved in Sunday school activities

_______**The Clown Ministry Handbook** **$7.95**
by Janet Litherland #DD-B163
The first and most complete text on the art of clown ministry

_______**Fundraising for Youth**
by Dorthy M. Ross #DD-B184
Hundreds of wonderful ways of raising funds for youth organizations

_______**Something for the Kids #DD-B192** **$6.95**
by Ted Lazicki
Fifty-two "front-row" sermons for children

_______**Youth Ministry from Start to Finish #DD-B193** **$7.95**
by Janet Litherland
A step-by-step approach to successful youth ministry

I understand that I may return any book for a full refund if not satisfied.

NAME: ____

ORGANIZATION NAME: ____________________________

ADDRESS: _____________________________________

CITY: ____________________ STATE: ________ ZIP: __________

PHONE: _______________________________________

☐ **Check Enclosed**
☐ **Visa or Master Card #** ___________________________

Signature: _____________________________________
(required for Visa/Mastercard orders)

COLORADO RESIDENTS: Please add 3% sales tax.

SHIPPING: Include $1.50 for the first book and 50¢ for each additional book ordered.

☐ *Please send me a copy of your complete catalog of books or plays.*

Banner Ideas:

Banner Ideas:

Banner Ideas: